ESSAY AND LECTURES

ON THE

INDUSTRIAL DEVELOPMENT OF INDIA

ESSAY AND LECTURES

ON THE

INDUSTRIAL DEVELOPMENT OF INDIA AND OTHER INDIAN SUBJECTS

[1880 -1906]

PRAMATHA NATH BOSE, B. SC. (LONDON), F. G. S.

GYAN

Published by

Gyan Publishing House
5, Ansari Road
Daryaganj, New Delhi-110002
Phone: 011-47034999, 9811692060
E-mail: books@gyanbooks.com

Distribution Network
gyanbooks.com
India, USA, Canada, UK, Australia, France

ISBN: 978-81-212-8714-2 (PB)
First Published, 1906

2nd Impression 2023

Printed at: Gyan Press, Delhi.

ESSAY AND LECTURES ON THE INDUSTRIAL DEVELOPMENT OF INDIA
Author: Pramatha Nath Bose

ESSAYS AND LECTURES

ON THE

INDUSTRIAL DEVELOPMENT OF INDIA

AND OTHER INDIAN SUBJECTS

[*1880-1906*]

BY

PRAMATHA NATH BOSE, B. SC. (LONDON), F.G.S.,

AUTHOR OF A "HISTORY OF HINDU CIVILISATION DURING BRITISH RULE"

Calcutta:

W. NEWMAN & CO.

1906.

Printed by Asutosh Chakraburti,
at the Elm Press, 62-2-1, *Beadon Street, Calcutta.*

CONTENTS

SECTION III.—Miscellaneous

SECTION I

INDUSTRIAL

CHAPTER I

Industrial Development of India

(Presidential Address at the Bengal Industrial Conference, 1891)

*   *   *   *   *

THE all but utter extinction of our industries has ruined our artisan classes. Down to the commencement of the present century we used to make enough clothes, not only to meet our own demands, but also to export a good portion of them. Our export trade then consisted mainly of manufactured cotton; now it consists almost exclusively of raw produce. In 1798-99, India exported to England one crore and-a-half worth of piece-goods; in 1888-89, we imported from England nearly 29 crores worth of manufactured cotton. The profits of manufacture which a century ago remained in the country and enriched it now swell the ever increasing drain to Europe. The greater majority of the artisan classes who once formed large flourishing communities have been driven to earn their subsistence as agriculturists or labourers. Mr. H. J. S. Cotton, Secretary to the Government of Bengal, says; "Not a year passes in which the commissioners and district officers do not bring to the notice of Government that the manufacturing classes from all parts of the country are becoming impoverished......Agriculture is everywhere expanding at the expense of manufacturing industry." Large towns with urban populations have dwindled into inconsiderable villages. It has been estimated that nearly ninety per cent of our population is now dependent upon agriculture. But, while our people have become so exclusively agricultural, the extent of cultivable land, in proportion to the population, is very small. Sir James Craird, an eminent agricultural authority, was greatly struck by this fact when he visited India as a Famine Commissioner in 1878. He says: "A square mile of land in England, cultivated highly, gives employment to fifty persons in the proportion of twenty-five men, young and old, and twenty-five women and boys. If four times the number, that is, two hundred, be allowed for each square mile of cultivated land in India, it would take up only one-third of the population." The pressure upon land has been gradually increasing. The time is not far distant when it will fail to meet the enhanced demand upon it, unless its food-growing capacity increases; and the prospect in that direction is certainly not cheering. The agricultural experiments which have been carried on by Government so long have not yet led to any important practical results. Dr. Voelcker, a renowned agriculturist, who was recently engaged by the Government to report upon the possible directions in which our agriculture may be improved, says after carefully inspecting nearly every part of India:—"I unhesitatingly dispose of the ideas which have been erroneously entertained, that the ryot's cultivation is primitive and backward, and say that nearly all the attempts made in the past to teach him have failed, because he understands far better than his would-be teachers the particular circumstances under which he has to pursue his calling." With regard to deep ploughing, Dr. Voelcker says: "Though there may be instances where deep ploughing would be effectual, I believe that in the great majority of cases the native system of ploughing is the one best adapted to the conditions; and that were a furrow-turning plough used, the result would be to lose a great deal of the precious moisture." So the out-look for our agricultural classes is indeed very gloomy. Large numbers of impoverished artisans have swelled their ranks, and struggle with them to earn a subsistence from land. That the struggle for existence amongst them is being gradually intensified, is indicated by many symptoms. It is the impression of many well-experienced men that the masses of our people are deteriorating in physique, and that they do not get sufficient sustenance to resist the attacks of fever. No doubt, here and there, we have flourishing well-to-do agricultural communities, as in Eastern Bengal. But over the greater portion of our country, in North-Western Bengal, Behar, the North-Western Provinces, Madras, Bombay, &c., the agricultural classes are far from prosperous; indeed, they are already much depressed. One season of drought is enough to produce widespread distress. Our labouring classes have also been largely recruited from the artisan population. They, too, are very hard pressed. It is true their wages have increased, but not in the same ratio as the price of food-grains. Three centuries ago, in the time of Akbar, we learn from that storehouse of the most valuable information, the *Ain i-Akbari*, that the wages of unskilled labourers, such as bamboo-cutters, &c., was $9\frac{3}{8}$ pies per day. But wheat then sold for about 5 annas per maund, and coarse rice for 8 annas per maund. Since then their wages have increased three—or even four-fold, but the prices for wheat and for coarse rice have increased sevenfold, so that labourers were nearly twice as comfortable in the time of Akbar as they are now. They must now go without not only the comforts which they then enjoyed, but in many cases without the bare necessaries of life also. Thus we find that our artisan classes have been well nigh ruined and that the struggle for existence amongst the agricultural and the labouring classes has been gradually intensified to a most appalling extent. The death-rate appears to have been increasing. In 1880 it was 20·98 per 1,000 ; in 1889 it was 28·05. No doubt there is always the suspicion that the registration may not have been efficient, and that the figures may not be reliable. Still so great an increase as 8 per thousand in 10 years can scarcely be due to inefficient registration in previous years.

The condition of the middle class is no better than that of the mass of the people ; probably it is worse. They are all but excluded from the higher grades of the Government services. Old customs like the joint-family system still continue to impose upon them very heavy pecuniary responsibilities. New customs have arisen which add seriously to those responsibilities ; these customs may be good, but they add to their encumbrances all the same. They have to work according to the exacting methods of Western civilisation: indeed, they have to work like Englishmen, but without an Englishman's food, without an Englishman's habits, and without an Englishman's reward. The cost of living has increased, but not the means to meet the increased cost. Meat diet is too expensive for the majority of them; milk and various preparation of milk, which form the chief articles of nutrition in our diet, have become very dear. So our middle classes have to work harder than ever upon diet less nutritious than our people were used to in days gone by. Without any scope for legitimate ambition in the Government services, they swell the ranks of hungry clerks and discontented newspaper writers. No wonder they grow up weak in body, and weak in mind; no wonder that such fell diseases as diabetes, etc., are counting their victims by scores. Western education is still confined to an inconsideracle portion of our population; not more than 1 in 2,500 of our people receive what is called advanced education. There is still a very wide field for its spread. But the struggle for existence amongst our educated class is already beginning to be very keenly and very widely felt. Thus we find that there is no section of our population that may be said to be prosperous. Our artisans, our peasants, our labourers, our educated classes, all are sunk in the lowest depths of poverty. The outlook for them all is equally gloomy. What then is the remedy?

The Government services can offer only a few drops of water amongst thirsty millions; can afford relief only to an insignificant fraction of our distressed population. I have again to ask, what then is the remedy? The only remedy that is likely to be of very wide application, that is likely to afford substantial relief to all classes of our people, is the development of our industries. It is industries alone that can relieve the distress of the mass of the people by lightening the pressure upon land; it is industries alone that can relieve the distress of our middle classes by affording them openings other than clerkships. The Government and the people are alike beginning to understand this. Some steps have already been taken in the Bombay Presidency by our more practical brethren the Parsis and the Mahrattas. The fact of so many of our educated friends having met at this Conference, and the recent establishment of a glass factory and of a cotton mill on a somewhat large scale in Bengal, by indigenous enterprise, show that we who have hitherto formed a community chiefly composed of clerks,—that we too have at last awakened to a proper sense of the gravity of our present situation.

This brings us, gentlemen, to the first topic which has been put down for discussion at this Conference, *vis.*, the Industrial Survey of the whole Province. Before we can suggest any remedy we must first know what industries are capable of revival or of expansion. Many such do no doubt occur to you. Cotton manufacture has a very wide field before it. In 1888-89 we imported some 29 crores worth of cotton piece-goods, yarn, thread, etc. There is no reason why we should not be able to make at least the greater portion of the cotton articles we require. A century ago, as I have already told you, we used to make not only all that we wanted for our own requirements, but were able also to export a large quantity to Europe. The iron industry also has a promising future before it. Then, there are various small industries, such as coal, petroleum, glass, soap, match, paper, pottery, sugar-refining, dyeing and tanning, which are likely to afford scope for enterprise.

The next question that is to engage our attention is, How are these industries to be developed? This brings us to the much talked-of topic of technical education, the second in the programme before us. In olden days, our artisan castes used to take care of our industries; the weaving castes looked after our cotton manufactures; the potters took care of our pottery; our tanning was in charge of *muchis* and *chamars*; and so forth. Ours was a very well ordered community : unaffected by ambition, contented with his lot, ignorant of every thing but his own calling—everybody was happy in his own sphere. He had plenty to eat, and had a large share of comforts also. The struggle for existence, and the restlessness and discontent which are the inevitable consequences of such struggle were then unknown. Each excelled in his own handicraft—the potter in pottery, the weaver in weaving, the dyer in dyeing; and he earned enough from his trade to make himself comfortable. But the good, old times have passed away. We may sigh for them, but they will never return. We must move with the times or perish. The progress of natural science in the western world has effected a revolution in industrial methods. The day of mere manual skill is gone by; and, rest assured, will never return. This revolution took us by surprise; we were not prepared for it; we were not given the time to prepare ourselves for it; and the result is that we are simply paralysed. Our caste system no doubt aided progress in the earlier stages of our civilisation; it has also served to maintain order for centuries since the decay of that civilisation. But caste has done so at the sacrifice of progress—I mean, progress such as it is undestood in Europe and America. It was not to be expected that illiterate weavers, or illiterate dyers, or illiterate miners, would apply the scientific methods of modern industries to their professions. Not having done so they have gone to the wall. Our upper classes have hitherto mainly received what may be called literary education. Many of us can speak the English language well, a few better even than many members of the House of Commons. We can turn out readable and entertaining novels and dramas, and able disquisitions on religion and philosophy; but, as for following the lead of the Europeans in the development of the resources of our country, we might, under the present circumstances, just as well think of flying to the moon. We have not had the necessary training. We see around us Europeans exploiting the mineral and other resources of our country, starting mills and factories, and we are bewildered. All the good the mines the mills and the factories do us is in the direction of affording employment to labourers among the mass of the people, and to clerks among the upper classes. Talk of our developing our resources! We do not even know what those resources are; we have not had the needful education. Ask our graduates where coal and petroleum are to be found in India? Under what conditions can they be worked to profit? How is iron smelted? How can soap be manufactured from indigenous materials ?—Not one in a thousand will be able to give anything like a satisfactory answer. Many there are who will intelligently discuss abstruse questions of philosophy; who will make apt quotations from Shakespeare, Milton, and a host of other poets; who have mastered English history better than many Englishmen; but few there are who know anything about the vast resources of their country, and how they can be utilised and developed.

Yes, technical education is very badly needed in this country. But what kind of technical education is it that we want? Technical education may be briefly defined to be a training for the industries. In order to settle what kind of technical education is specially wanted, we must find out what industries are capable of special development. Now, industries may be grouped under two heads:—(1) *Art-Industries*, such as carpentry, shoe-making, engraving, modelling etc., that is to say, industries which have a very remote, if any, connection with science. (2) *Science-Industries*, industries more or less dependent upon some branch or other of natural science, such as mining, glass-manufacture, cotton-manufacture, soap-making, tanning, &c. From what I have already said, it will be apparent that it is the science and not the art-industries that require to be specially developed. There is not much room for expansion in the petty industries, such as carpentry, tailoring, shoe-making, etc. As I wrote in the *Calcutta Review* about four years ago (January, 1888) " It is not the making up of cloth, so much as the manufacture of cloth, that is more particularly wanted in this country. Few people are in a position to use made-up clothes at all, far less clothes of fine cut or nice fit, or boots and shoes of approved shape and fashionable make. Of furniture of any kind there is but little demand. Our wants in these directions are at best extremely limited; and they are, we think, well enough supplied at present. Besides, such technical training as is needed for the handicrafts could, we believe, be best obtained at the existing shops. Whatever field there is for enterprise in them is being occupied, as witnessed by the tailor's shops of Chitpore-road, and the cabinet-ware houses of Bow Bazar."

With regard to Indian Art, its fate is doomed. Any attempt to revive it, at least on a large scale, is destined to fail. A society has been lately formed in England under very high auspices for the encouragement of Indian art. We must be thankful to our English friends for it. But, I am afraid, it will not do much good. The demand for Indian art is daily decreasing, and will continue to decrease as the price of labour rises. In these days of cheap imitations, genuine art productions, requiring a vast amount of labour, are not likely to hold their own. Cheap cloth, cheap iron, cheap paper, cheap glass, cheap soap, in short, cheap necessaries of life, are what we particularly want; and these will, therefore, command a large sale. It is the larger industries, involving scientific methods and appliances, what are called science-industries, such as cotton, glass, iron, paper, etc., which are most likely to develop the resources of the country and make it rich, and which are therefore specially needed. With cheap labour and raw materials in abundance, there is every reason to expect, that these manufactures will be remunerative.

It is thus evident that the sort of technical education which we specially stand in need of, should be such as will fit us for the science-industries. Gentlemen, we find schools rising here and there, where a little carpentry, a little watch repairing, a little tailoring, or a little modelling is taught, which are dignified with the name of technical schools. I do not mean to say that such technical schools are absolutely without their use. But do not be deluded with the idea that they are the sort of technical schools we specially require, or that they will develop the resources of the country to any appreciable extent. They are not likely to do much good to the country, and may do considerable harm, inasmuch as their establishment may create the erroneous impression in the public mind, that real technical education is spreading whereas, in reality, it is not. We must not be deceived by shadows, but must endeavour to get at the real substance. I have heard of an institution where watches were repaired (I don't know whether properly or not), clothes were made up, and a few articles of furniture were made. This institution, going forth to the public with the pompous name of a Technical School, managed to secure some pecuniary contributions. Our public should know that this is not the kind of technical school we want, that this kind of technical education will not develop our industries, at least to any perceptible extent.

Having decided what kind of technical education is needed, the next more important and more difficult question is how and where it is to be imparted. This is a matter which requires to be thoroughly discussed. To start an independent Technological Institute will be a very costly affair. Though the expense, however great, will be fully repaid, and will be quite justifiable, our Government, under existing circumstances, will probably grudge it; and I see no chance of the necessary money being raised by private subscriptions. Two or three lacs will be nowhere. The problem before us, at least for the present, would be how to utilise the existing Government institutions such as the Sibpore, the Roorki and the Presidency Colleges, the Government Railway workshops and the Government factories, for the purposes of technical education. The establishment of the chair of Geology at the Presidency College is a step in advance; the progress and dissemination of scientific education will further the cause of technical education, for the latter is based upon the former. We need feel no hesitation in approaching the Government for help either in the matter of technical education or in any other matter affecting the development of our industries. The declared policy of our Government is the promotion of our industries. In his address to the Delhi Municipality in 1881, Lord Ripon said:—"Yes, gentlemen, we do desire to avail ourselves of the assistance of native industry to the utmost possible extent; . . . . it is a part of our policy that we should endeavour to encourage industry, and develop it to the utmost of our power." In every civilised country, technical education receives large and liberal Government support. I am afraid, as I have already told you, that we cannot expect our Government to go to the expense of founding independent technical institutes. But any scheme involving a moderate outlay for the furtherance of technical education, by a slight modification or a slight expansion of existing institutions, may be reasonably pressed upon the attention of the Government.

After settling how technical education is to be imparted the next and still more important question is, how are industries to be started. This brings us to the fourth topic in our programme, *viz.*, how best to promote the joint-stock system in this country, in connection with industrial undertakings. No industry now-a-days is likely to be remunerative unless started on a large scale, which means large outlay; and it is of no use to give technical education unless such industries be started. Ours is a very poor country. Still by joint-stock organisation sufficient capital could be raised for the successful starting of many large industries. A beginning has already been made in this direction. The recent establishment of a glass manufacturing company and of a cotton weaving company in Bengal is a very hopeful sign. I have no doubt more companies will be gradually formed. It is possible that in a few cases the success at the commencement may not quite come up to our expectations, but it is better far that it should be so,—nay, that we should even have a few failures than that we should make no endeavour to march in the path of progress.

Gentlemen, the task before us is a very difficult one. The extension of railways and the absence of a protective tariff of any sort have not only contributed to the ruin of our industries, but have also placed very serious difficulties in the way of their revival. We are all jubilant over the extension of railways. They have certainly added greatly to the comforts of travelling. But they have done a little harm also. If they have helped to mitigate the horrors of famines, they have also partly helped to cause them. For, by carrying European wares cheaply into the interior, they have been one of the contributory causes of the destruction of our industries; and the destruction of indigenous industries means increased pressure upon land. We who have received our education in English schools are imbued with ideas of free trade as much as English people are, or possibly more so. But it is time we should re-consider our ideas on the subject. I will let an Englishman, a high official of the Government of Bengal, Mr. H. J. S. Cotton, speak on it. He says :—

" Another suggestion of even more practical character is that the Government of this country should afford assistance to indigenous industries by protection. We were told in a recent official report, with an air of exultation, that India sets an example to the whole civilised world in the matter of free trade. But is it to the advantage of India itself that it should do so? This is a wide question, and I cannot pursue at this late hour the discussions to which it gives rise. Different authorities will have different opinions on it, but my brief analysis of the decay of Indian manufactures will have prepared you to expect my own personal conclusion, that the time is ripe for a careful consideration of current convictions on this subject." Every civilised country except England has its protection-tariffs. India is, I believe, the only country which has to admit foreign manufactures without any protective duty. It will, however, be futile to expect our Government to impose any duties which may even remotely partake of the nature of protection. Such protection as is needed for our present or future industries—and infant industries do require protection—must be given by us. The question for us to settle is, how is that to be done? Sometime ago I heard that a Joint Stock Company was to be formed on a large scale for the sale of articles of indigenous manufacture. The idea is a good one, and I hope it will be carried out. I have no doubt it will indirectly afford some amount of protection.

Gentlemen, very serious difficulties beset our path. Our efforts to overcome them should be all the more earnest and all the more energetic. We must "awake, arise, or be for ever fallen." Believe me, gentlemen, unless we exert ourselves immediately, there will be scarcely any room left for us. I do not wish to detract from the value of social or political reform; but industrial reform has to me a value far higher than either, What will social or political reform avail a starving nation? And starvation does stare us in the face in the near future. A nation of half-starved clerks and coolies and cultivators will never make any sound progress. We may, and often do, make a show of progress; but substantial progress there will be none until we are in a position to make railways and to work mines and mills on a large scale.

CHAPTER II

INDUSTRIAL DEVELOPMENT BY INDIAN ENTERPRISE

(Lecture delivered in Calcutta, July 1906)

THE recent industrial awakening of India, indications of which are noticeable on all sides, must fill the heart of every well-wisher of hers with joy and hope. Exhibitions of indigenous manufactures which ten years ago were few and far between, are now held every year in many important districts, and the Exhibition in connection with the Indian National Congress has now become an annual institution. An industrial conference was held last year which, well organised and well managed, is capable of accomplishing very useful work. The Swadeshi movement which has been in existence for the last quarter of a century, but which hitherto has met with but little favour, has since last year received a great impetus, and now promises to be a motive force in industrial development. Fifteen years ago, appeals for funds for the promotion of technical education in Bengal met with but little response, were, in fact, a cry in the wilderness. But within the last two years funds amounting to not less than ten lakhs of rupees have been raised for the purpose in Bengal alone.

The industrial awakening is most marked in Bengal. It was certainly most needed there. Bengal has taken a leading part in recent intellectual, religious, and social progress. But, in respect of industrial enterprise she has hitherto been far more backward than Bombay or even the Punjab and the United Provinces. Cotton manufacture, the principal industry of the Western Presidency, is largely, if not mainly, financed and managed by the people of that Presidency. On the other hand, Jute manufacture and coal mining, the two chief industries of Bengal, an almost exclusively in the hands of Europeans. The people of Bengal are, however, now adopting vigorous measures to make up for their past neglect, and it seems now as if her industrial backwardness will soon be a thing of the past. A cotton mill has just been acquired by a Bengali Joint Stock Company; improved handlooms are being extensively introduced; a Bengali pottery concern is about to expand its operations with up-to--date equipment; a joint stock coal concern due mainly to Bengali enterprise has been started this year; and talks about the establishment of match, soap and other industries on a small scale are gradually crystallising into action.

A good start is being made, and if this newborn enterprise be well directed, it cannot fail to be fruitful of very important and very great results. Hitherto, the development of the economic resources of India has been effected mainly by Europeans. The mineral resources especially have been exploited almost exclusively by them. Within the ten years (1894 to 1903) the output of manganese ores has increased about fifteen times (from 11,410 to 165,006 tons); that of petroleum has increased more than seven fold (from 11,452,649 to 87,859,069 gallons); that of mica has very nearly quadrupled (285 to 1077 tons); that of gold has trebled from 210,412 to 603,218 ounces; and that of coal has more than doubled—from 2,823,907 to 7,438,386 tons. In regard to the manufacturing industries, within the last 24 years (1881-82 to 1904-05), the number of Jute mills has nearly trebled (8 to 22); that of mills for wool, silk, hemp &c. has increased more than ten times (3 to 31); that of paper mills has increased five fold (1 to 5); and that of sugar factories has more than doubled (4 to 9). But indigenous enterprise has had very little share in this industrial expansion. At the end of the financial year 1904-1905, the nominal capital of the joint stock companies engaged in mining ventures is given as as 3,79,54,000 rupees. I doubt if even a fiftieth part of this capital is contributed by my countrymen. A company for the manufacture of steel and iron on modern methods is about to be floated with a capital of a crore and a half of rupees. The difficulty of raising it in India has compelled its promoters, themselves Indians, to form the company in England.

It will be thus seen, that the field of larger industries is mostly occupied by Europeans; and the new-born Indian enterprise will have to face the keenest competition with them. The Europeans have some highly important advantages on their side. They belong to the richest community in the world, the Indians to the poorest. Capital is so abundant in Europe, that it is satisfied with a return of 3 or 4 per cent, but treble this amount would hardly tempt the investment of Indian capital in any undertaking which is attended with any risk. The Europeans have had a start of half a century in higher technical education, whereas the Indians have only just awakened to the imperative necessity of such education in industrial development on modern methods. The number of educated Indians who know anything, and until lately who cared anything about the economic resources of their country is small ; and that of those who know how they should be developed is still smaller. The Europeans have learnt the utility of co-operation, so that there is hardly any large business undertaken by them which is not managed on joint stock principles ; on the other hand, the Indians generally are just appreciating the advantages of co-operation in industrial ventures. For instance, in 1904, there were 110 petty collieries worked by nearly as many private owners, almost all of them Indians. Each of these collieries has its small staff (whatever their qualifications may be), its workshop &c., and in many cases a separate railway siding. On the other hand, there were 142 collieries worked by only 41 joint stock companies almost all of which are European. The output of the 110 privately owned collieries was only 786,670 tons, a comparatively insignificant fraction of the total production of the 142 collieries owned by joint stock companies, which was as much as 6,277,010 tons. If the owners of the 110 petty collieries were actuated by a spirit of co-operation, and if some of them combined and amalgamated their properties when they adjoined each other, the management would be far more efficient and economical than it is at present, and there would be a larger margin for profit, so that they would not have to live from hand to mouth as they mostly do at present.

Besides the comparative scarcity of capital, the inadequacy of technical training and lack of the amount of co-operation requisite for large undertakings, there is another and probably a more potent cause which stands in the way of industrial development—the hereditary aversion of the higher castes for trades and industries which have hitherto been relegated to the lower, and, in some cases, to the very lowest classes of the Indian society. There has always existed more or less of such aversion in all civilized communities. It was very pronounced among the ancient Greeks. But, in the West the line of demarcation between the industrial and other classes has now been almost entirely effaced. In fact, the modern civilisation of the West is essentially an industrial civilisation. On the contrary, in India, it is only now, that attempts are being made to bridge the gulf which the caste-system has hitherto interposed between the trading and manufacturing classes on the one hand and the higher and intellectually superior classes on the other. The divorce of intellect from art and manufacture is to no small extent responsible for the decadence of our industries. While it is hardly desirable that the industrial spirit should be so dominant here as it is in the West, we cannot expect sound industrial progress unless our higher classes imbibe a little more of that spirit than they have done hitherto, and shake off their constitutional indifference for trades and industries.

The Permanent Settlement, though it has unquestionably done a deal of good in other ways, has, I am inclined to think, been rather prejudicial to the industrial advancement of my Bengali compatriots. Land has hitherto been the main object of investment with the well-to-do portion of our community. I think one of the reasons why the Western Presidency has got an aristocracy of merchants is that it has not got an aristocracy of Zamindars. However, our Zamindars are now largely interesting themselves in industrial movements, and it is confidently hoped that what has hitherto stood in the way of industrial enterprise will now help it forward.

Under the circumstances, Indian enterprise is generally taking the easier direction of the smaller industries such as tanning and the manufacture of soap, perfumes &c. But it is hardly necessary to point out, that it should aim high and not rest satisfied with turning out articles which, though important, cannot add very materially to the wealth of country. Besides, the line of demarcation between the smaller and the larger industries is not very sharp. Without descending into details, it may be stated generally, that there are some in the former category which would be more remunerative if conducted on a large than on a small scale.

The prosecution of the smaller industries would no doubt, afford a good training for larger and more hazardout undertakings. But we must bear in mind, that time is a very important consideration. European enterprise is so watchful and alert, that it will not leave the economic resources of India to be exploited by the Indians when they are ready to do so. Manganese mining, for instance, was hardly known in India in the eighties. It has been started and developed within the last fifteen years—developed so fully indeed, that under existing conditions, it hardly offers a tempting field for the newborn enterprise of my countrymen. One must now-a-days be wideawake and seize industrial opportunities quickly or they are lost to him, perhaps for ever. The eastern mind cannot quite grasp the why or wherefore of this breathless race for industrial progress, this ceaseless struggle for the accumulation of wealth. The spirit of the modern civilisation of the west does not quite harmonise with the spirit of the Indian civilisation. But if the Indians must take their proper share in the development of the resources of their country (and on that point there does not appear to be any difference of opinion now), they must adapt themselves to their environment, and cast themselves into the whirl of Western industrialism.

One of the most gratifying results of the recent national movement has been the development of a spirit of self-reliance. But we must see that self-reliance does not degenerate into conceit. There are some matters—spiritual development, for instance,—in which we can dispense with foreign help. There are other matters, however, in which it would be suicidal not to seek and take such help. Industrial development is pre-eminently one of these. The mills, factories, and mines conducted by foreigners should serve as so many object lessons.

I have pointed out the disadvantages which my countrymen have to contend with in competing with Europeans. It is, however, very cheering that efforts are being made to overcome them, and with determined perseverance, there is no reason why the efforts should not be crowned with success. The fact that no less than six joint stock Bengali Companies have been floated this year in Bengal speaks volumes in favour of the earnestness of the educated community of that province.

An industrial movement was set on foot by Bengali enterprise fifteen years ago. But the time was not ripe then, and it failed. Of the seven or eight joint stock concerns which were the outcome of that movement only one or two have survived. The failures must not dishearten us, but we must extract lessons of wisdom from them. I have been keenly watching the industrial development of my country for the last quarter of a century, and I may say without the least hesitation, that the present movement is inaugurated under far more hopeful conditions than the one that preceded it, and with careful piloting, there is no reason why the Indians should not be able to overcome the difficulties with which they are confronted. The attitude of the Government towards indigenous enterprise now, whatever it may have been in the earlier years of British Rule, is decidedly favourable, nay even sympathetic. The *swadeshi* movement, if it be well-organised, and well-directed, cannot fail to exercise a most beneficial influence; and in competing with Europeans there are some advantages on the Indian side which must not be overlooked. The comparatively lower scale of wages which satisfies an Indian is a point which is greatly in his favour. It is true that low wage does not necessarily imply low cost of production. But with the spread of technical education, the higher class of Indian labour is expected to be more efficront than it is at present, and efficient labour at a comparatively low wage is a decidedly favourable point in competition. The Zamindars of Bengal and the chiefs of the Native States own between them a very considerable proportion of land containing the richest mineral resources, and enjoy, therefore, special opportunities for developing them, as indeed, they do for developing also various agricultural industries. It is regrettable that these opportunities have been but little availed of hitherto. It is to be hoped, however, that better use will be made of them in the future.

The industrial development of India offers to the Indians a vast, at present almost boundless field for action. It would relieve the pressure upon land which has of late been intensified by the extinction of indigenous industries, open out promising avenues of employment to our middle classes, and diminish the economic drain from India. There is also another consideration. I do not wish to minimise the importance of political agitation in civilised countries. But situated as India is, her efforts in that direction must be more or less of the nature of appeals to the moral sense of England, There is no indication, however, that that sense has as yet been developed to the extent which would make it a motive factor in practical politics. In fact, so far as the treatment of the weaker peoples of the world is concerned, the ethical standard of the west instead of being elevated appears lately to have been perceptibly lowered. The aggressive imperialism of modern Europe is based upon industrialism. It is chiefly in the interests of their industries, that the greater powers of the west are anxious to dominate the peoples of the East. If these peoples made a vigorous, well concerted effort to develop their resources on western methods, and supply their own wants, their markets would cease to be exploited in the way they now are by western manufactures, and their lands would cease to be the happy hunting ground of western enterprise. Western imperialism, would thus die a natural and peaceful death, at least in its present highly objectionable militant form. That is a revolution so wholesome and far-reaching in its effects—wholesome and far-reaching in the interests both of the East and of the West—that it is well worth a mighty effort on the part of all orientals.

CHAPTER III

A Plea for a Patriotic Movement

(*National Magazine, May 1903*)

INDIA has now been under the domination and tutelage of one of the most highly civilised nations of the West for over a century. Yet, the fact is striking, that she should have so signally failed to imbibe the essential spirit of Western Civilisation and should present such a deplorable dearth of indigenous enterprise, whether engineering, manufacturing, agricultural or mining. All her railways, with but few insignificant exceptions, have been constructed with British material and British capital, and are under British management. All the more important mills and factories, with the exception of a few cotton mills in the Bombay Presidency and the Central Provinces, are in British hands, and the mineral resources of the country may be said to be almost exclusively exploited by foreigners.

It cannot be said that the Indians are wanting in assimilative faculty. Like the Chinese, they have inherited an ancient civilisation; but unlike their celestial brethren, they are not so blindly infatuated with it as to be insensible to the good or the useful side of any other. The absence of industrial enterprise is probably more marked in Bengal than in any other part of India; yet English education has made the greatest progress in that province, and all the more important reforms on Western lines which have been introduced into India within the last half century have been initiated and developed there. The foundation of the Theistic Church was laid in Bengal; the widow-remarriage movement began there; and the crusade against the caste-system, which has lain like an incubus on the Hindu social structure for so many centuries, has been carried out more vigorously and more effectively there than in any other province. Bengal boasts of orators who would by no means be unworthy of winning laurels on British platforms, of authors of no mean repute, and of legal luminaries who have adorned the highest tribunals in India, but she cannot point to a single individual who has made his mark in the industrial world, or to a single company which has successfully carried on any industrial enterprise, mining, manufacturing, or even agricultural, on a scale comparable to the operations of a third rate company in the West.

Nor can apathy be reasonably urged as an explanation of the lack of such enterprise, though the people are often taunted with it. It is true, that inheriting a, civilization, which, like all other ancient civilizations, is essentially non-industrial, looks down upon all money-making occupations, and leaves the pursuit of trades and industries to the lower castes, the educated community of India for a long time, while assimilating Western culture, did not take at all kindly to Western industrialism. But, the pressure of the annually increasing struggle for existence has left them no option; and during the last two decades, they have exhibited unmistakeable symptoms of a keen desire for the industrial development of their country on Western lines, not only by establishing associations and holding conferences and exhibitions, but also by attempting a good many industries on the joint-stock principle. In Bengal, for instance, the last decade of the last century, witnessed the rise and collapse of an indigenous cotton mill, two match factories, one glass factory, and of a mining company, not to speak of several less important concerns. The condition of the educated community is, indeed, pitiable. The great majority of them earn their livelihood as clerks, teachers, &c.; and keen competition has kept down their pittances to the figures which ohtained a quarter of a century, or even half a century ago. But within that time not only have the prices of nearly all the articles of the simple food on which they manage to subsist doubled or quadrupled, but by an irony of fate, Western Civilisation has insinuated itself into their ranks, and they have developed tastes which they have not the means to gratify. Even if their wants had not increased, their situation would have been embarrassing enough; but, with increased wants, it becomes quite insupportable. No wonder, then, that they should be eagerly casting about for, more promising avenues of employment than the well-beaten tracks of barren clerkdom; and what could be more promising than those that have led the Western nations to the pinnacle of material greatness?

The Government of India, whatever their policy in bye-gone times may have been, appear now to be not unfavourable to indigenous industrial development. They are confronted with a serious and rather entangled problem—How to prevent, or at least mitigate the rigour of Famine which has of late been recurring with such frequency that it may almost be said to have become chronic, and which may spell ruin to an increasingly expensive Western administration carried on with the diminishing means of an indigent Eastern population. It is not surprising, therefore, that the Government should have of late shown some desire to bring the agricultural methods of the country more in harmony with those pursued in the West in order that the yield from the land might be increased, and also to relieve the excessive pressure upon agriculture due primarily to the extinction of the indigenous industries, by fitting the people for modern industrial pursuits. Nor has the Governmental desire in these directions altogether evaporated in the exuberant verbiage of portly reports, but has sometimes even crystallised into solid action. We have the provincial departments of agriculture and the experimental farms; and the Government of Bengal for several years sent some of the most promising graduates of the Calcutta University to go through a course of agricultural education at Cirencester. The position of the Government is a difficult one. On the one hand, the industrial development of India by the Indians on Western methods and on Western scale would deal a blow to the manufacturing prosperity of Great Britain; on the other hand, it is only by such development that the impoverishment of the people could be prevented, and the danger of the Government becoming bankrupt could be averted. No wonder then that they—on the hypothesis of course of the subordination of Indian to British interests—should so far have been so lukewarm, and should have confined what little action they have taken hitherto to agriculture which does not in any way clash with British interests, but, on the contrary rather favours them. But though the Government have not yet done anything actively to promote and foster native enterprise, they have certainly not placed any obstacles—at least any serious ones—in its way.

What, then, are the causes of this lack of indigenous enterprise?

One of the essential conditions of industrial development on modern methods is capital. Concentration of capital is the most striking feature of Western industry. The introduction of labour-saving machinery has effected a revolution in the industrial world. The success of an industry now depends upon the scale and the quality of machinery used in it. No industry on a small scale can be sufficiently remunerative under present conditions. The more gigantic the operations and the more extensive the employment of machinery, or in other words, the larger the capital, the more assured will the success of an industry be. And there are some industries like cotton manufacture, iron smelting, &c., which can not even be started successfully without a large capital. The competition in them is so keen, and the margin of profit so small, that they cannot be remunerative unless they are run on an enormous scale with the most improved machinery and on the most approved methods. This is much to be regretted. Capitalism, which leads to Mammonism, is probably the greatest curse of modern civilisation, and the Western philosophers have not been slow to condemn its manifest and manifold evils, though being born and bred in their midst they do not see them quite so plainly as we Asiatics do from a distance. But all the same, capitalism is increasing at a tremendously rapid pace just like militarism the evils of which are quite as plain and as vehemently denounced; and we must move on with the times or perish, even though such "progress" may clash with our long and fondly cherished moral ideals.

This fact, then, the necessity of large capital, must be impressed upon the enterprising youth of India. We can hardly realise without straining our imagination the gigantic industrial investments of the West. It would probably be no exaggeration to say, that the hoarded wealth of all the wealthy potentates of Hindusthan would barely make up the capital employed by a single great Trust of America.

Whether India is being gradually impoverished or not, it is admittedly one of the poorest countries even in Asia. How is she then to provide the capital necessary to compete with the wealthy West? Ninety per cent. of her population eke out a precarious subsistance from agriculture and are so exhausted by repeated famines, that a good many of them have not the means to tide over a single season of exceptional drought; of the remaining ten per cent., the greater majority are not much better off; and many among them belonging to the higher castes have to keep up an appearance of gentility on pittances which would hardly keep together the body and soul of a British workman. There is a small minority of business-men, bankers and merchants who are rich, at least in the Indian sense. But, in the first place, they have generally not received the stimulus of Western education, and though enterprising enough in their accustomed grooves have no conception of industrial ventures of the Western world. In the second place, they find such secure and profitable investments ready to hand for what capital they command, that they would not risk it on any of an uncertain and speculative character. In a country where capital is so scarce that an interest of nine per cent. is the usual return for the safest possible investment, is it any wonder that it should not be forthcoming for enterprises which barely pay a dividend of five per cent.? Yet, even the remote prospect of such a dividend, and that too in distant countries would be enough to tempt the capital of Western capitalists, so overburdened are they with a superfluity of that commodity, and so strongly are they impelled by a burning desire to augment it. There are, it is true, a few Rajas and Zamindars who, if they were so minded, might subscribe among themselves sufficient capital to gradually float a few industries on a befitting scale. But in addition to a general want of high Western education which they share with the capitalist classes just mentioned, they entertain a deep-rooted hereditary antipathy to industrial occupations—an antipathy which until recently influenced people of their rank even in the West where the levelling tendencies of a commercial civilisation have been at work for nearly a century.

The want of capital is, indeed, a serious obstacle in the way of the industrial regeneration of India, the formidable nature of which is not as a rule adequately grasped.

Another important factor of modern industrial progress is technical education—not the education given in the so-called technical schools which have of late sprung up in various parts of India, and in which carpentary, and similar petty trades are taught, but the education based upon Natural Science which is imparted in the technical institutes of Europe. Western civilisation is based upon Natural Science, as the Eastern is upon Mental and Moral Science; and if I had any choice between the two, I would unhesitatingly decide in favour of the latter. The practical applications of Natural Science have wrought incalculable mischief especially to the peoples outside the pale of Western civilisation; and in my opinion, they, on the whole, have proved rather a curse than a blessing to humanity. It is steam and electricity, and the numerous infernal compounds invented by Chemistry, which enable the greater Powers of the West to deprive the weaker peoples of the world of their independence and to exploit and enslave them. The weak have been more or less exploited by the strong in all ages and all over the globe, but never so scientifically, and, therefore, so systematically, so universally and so relentlessly.

But, the Asiatics have no choice. They must march with the Western progress or perish. Japan is the only country in the East which has clearly perceived this, and that has been her saving. If she, like China, had remained obstinately blind to the wonderful progress which Natural Science has made in the West, she wou'd not have been, as she now is, courted as an ally or treated as an equal, but would probably have been smarting under the blow of the "mailed fist" or some European Power.

The Indians must thoroughly grasp this fact—the paramount importance of Natural Science in modern civilisation which is essentially industrial. Their education must be more of a scientific and less of a literary character. They need not feel any compunction of conscience in devoting themselves heart and soul to the study of the practical applications of Natural Science. For, the objective in their case is not, and never will be, Imperial Expansion, but the harmless exploitation of the resources of their own country. There should be well-organised and well-equipped institutions all over the country for imparting high education in Science and its applications. There are but few such at present. Here, again the excessive poverty of the people stands in the way. Scientific and technical education is very costly. Many lacs would be required to equip and endow even a single modest institution for such education. But, the Government, though they may fully recognise its necessity in speeches and resolutions will be loth to substantially increase their educational expenditure ; and of the people the few that are able to contribute are either too ignorant to comprehend the value of Scientific and higher technical education, or too much demoralised to help to promote objects which are not calculated to win additions to their honours or appendages to their names. There are certainly very few who are likely to follow the noble example of the patriotic Tata in his munificent gift for a Research Instisute.

The third essential condition for industrial development in its early stage is Protection. It would be as irrational to demand the first attempts by one of the poorest, and so far as mechanical progress is concerned, one of the most backward peoples of the world to compete freely with the gigantic operations of the wealthiest peoples of the globe with a century of mechanical progress at their back, as it would be to expect a weak starveling to run a race successfully with an able-bodied athlete who has had the start of a league. In fact, industries require to be nursed, and even indulgently treated, just as children have to be ; and as in the one case, so in the other, free and unrestricted competition would result in death. In the West, with all its wealth and mechanical advancement, protection in some sh pe or other is found in every country except England. Even in England, her industries had to be protected and nurtured for a long time before they were enabled to withstand the competition of the world ; and as old age is second childhood, the adoption of some form of protection may be found necessary there in no very remote future for successful competition with younger and more vigorous rivals. But even should England ever have recourse to such a policy at home, it is highly improbable that she will ever extend it to this country as that would seriously clash with her self-interest as it is usually understood. The attitude of the Government in this respect was made quite clear in 1896, when low cotton duties were re-imposed. Highly moderate as they are, they could not be imposed without a counterveiling excise on indigenous cotton manufactures of such standards as are likely to compete with those of Manchester, and without an assurance to Lancashire that they would be repealed as soon as the financial position of India became satisfactory. "Though that will not be before the Greek Calends," observes Mr. S. S. Thorburn in a lecture delivered before the Fabian Society sometime ago, "We shall probably a few years hence, if not sooner, see strong pressure put upon the Secretary of State for India to insist once more upon the abolition of the duties. If so, there will again be serious risk that the interests of India may be subordinated to the electioneering manœvring of one or both of the parties bidding for power in England." Not only is there no possibility of the Government ever protecting Indian industries against Western, or at least English, competition, but they are even occasionally hampered to some extent. To give an instance from Mr. Thorburn's lecture to which I have just referred, "Some years ago," says Mr. Thorburn, "the cotton spinning and certain other industries in this country, having discovered I suppose, that Indians worked on Sundays, had their consciences awakened to the habitual desecration of the Sabbath out there. It was contended that as Sunday was a holy day in England, it should at least be a compulsory holiday for factory hands in India. The agitation had considerable support. In due course, the Secretary for India sent a despatch to the Government of India drawing attention to the sin of Sabbath-breaking in India, and calling on him *qua* factory hands, to conform to the rule in England, or give reason for not doing so. Amongst others, I was consulted for and against compulsory closing on Sundays. I suggested, that as Indians were mostly Hindus and Mahomedans, and invariably abstained from work on their own holy days, were Sundays also added, it would hardly be worth while to keep factories open at all, as the working days in the year would be reduced to something like two hundred in all. I hinted—no doubt indiscreetly, as we should not judge others—that probably the cotton-spinners of England had initiated the Sunday closing movement for India more from business than religious or sympathetic motives."

In the case of the first attempt at industrial development the three conditions we have mentioned above are of co-ordinate importance : capital is of no avail without technical education to utilise it advantageously, and *vice versa* ; and struggling industry the result of the union of capital and mechanical skill will be prematurely withered away if not carefully nursed and protected.

The absence of these essential conditions renders the prospects of indigenous industrial development in India very dark. Indeed, the circumstances are so very adverse, that the wonder is not that there is so little of indigenous enterprise, but that so many attempts should have been made. Without capital to speak of, without higher technical education worth the name, and without protection in any form, Young India is more to be pitied than censured for its lack of industrial enterprise.

What then is to be done ? Are the people of India

to sit with folded hands and be starved to extinction or to a condition of savagery whence they emerged thousands of years ago? As we have seen above, they cannot expect much help from their Government, and they must work out their own salvation themselves or perish.

The problem is a difficult and complicated one. There is, however, one solution of it which appears to me to be possible, and I shall close this article by briefly indicating it.

A movement has been going on for sometime past in different parts of India which is known as the *Swadeshi* (or Patriotic) movement. Its object being protection of indigenous industries, it is not much favoured by the generality of the more highly educated Indians who are imbued with the doctrine of Free Trade imparted with English education. When they, however, awaken to a sense of the fallacious nature of that doctrine when applied irrespective of surrounding circumstances, as I have no doubt they will soon, they will not only cease to look askance at this hitherto obscure and little recognised movement, but will perceive in it the germ of a great organisation which, if well directed, may effect the industrial regeneration of India.

A great central organisation with branches in all important towns having for its object the promotion of the interests of indigenous manufactures will go a long way towards at least a partial solution of the complicated problem of Indian industrial development. Such a movement will need in its apostles the exercise of even greater energy, greater patriotism, and greater self-sacrifice than the National Congress. They will have to lead a life devoid of the glamour which attaches to political pursuits, to preach upon subjects which would be considered tame when compared to those which (naturally enough) evoke the enthusiasm of orators and audiences in political meetings, to raise and administer immensely vaster funds than what suffices to set the machinery of the Congress going, and to set examples to their countrymen by eschewing foreign luxuries and being content with humbler garments and humbler fare than what they have hitherto been accustomed to. A properly organisd *Swadeshi* movement will demonstrate even more forcibly than the National Congress, that the apparently heterogeneous peoples of India are capable of uniting for the common good of their country. It would do for struggling industries in India what is done for them by Governments in independent countries by bounties and tariffs. If it can raise sufficient funds by enlisting the sympathy of the rich, it may bring technical education within its sphere of action, and well equipped technical institutes may be started under its auspices. What little capital there is in the country, if it does not respond to the impulse of patriotism infused into it by the *Swadeshi* movement, would on purely business considerations seek for investment in ventures which trained hands are ready to start, and for which there is the assurance of protection when started.

The idea of such an organisation may at present appear to many as chimerical. But there is really no reason why it should not be realised if a few earnest, capable, self-sacrificing men make it the mission of their lives. What is needed is a clear consideration of its urgent necessity, and a firm conviction that without the fostering care and watchful vigilance of some such organisation, the industrial enterprises of Young India will be unsuccessful and infructuous.

CHAPTER IV

THE POSSIBILITIES OF HANDLOOM WEAVING IN INDIA

(*Hindusthan Review, February, 1906*)

THE handloom industry has of late been attracting considerable public attention. It is a very important factor in the industrial regeneration of India; and its possibilities are unquestionably great. But they are capable of exaggeration; and, as a matter of fact, I find they are being exaggerated in some quarters to the detriment of the development of the mill industry. Mr. E. B. Havell, in a paper read at the Industrial Conference held at Benares, scouts the proposal for meeting the textile requirements of India by starting mills, and hardly thinks, "that those who make the suggestion have realised the economic and industrial bearings of the problem they attempt to solve." Still more recently in a letter published in the *Statesman* he predicts "that before many years have passed Science will have discovered some more artistic applications of mechanical force than those which condemn so many European artisans to lives of hopeless misery and degradation," and asks " is it a wise and statesmanlike policy to break up the organisation of Indian village industries and encourage Indian artisans to herd together in crowded factories when perhaps in a few decades Science will enable the Indian villagers to use mechanical power as easily as the capitalist does now ?"

The evils of western industrialism have long been patent. It has been fervently denounced by many an occidental philosopher—by Huxley, Wallace and Spencer among others in England. But there is no sign yet of the consummation so confidently predicted by Mr. Havell and so devoutly wished for by all Asiatics, who are being mercilessly exploited by the great powers of the West in the interests of their industries. In fact, "it seems to us an almost inexplicable enigma, that western writers, while they earnestly deprecate capitalism, should be blind to the principal cause which promotes it; so much so, indeed, that they often further it by their own action. The same physicist or chemist who will in his study or on the platform anathematise the capitalists for their iniquitous conduct will, perhaps, in his laboratory invent some machinery or discover some compound which will feed and fatten the capitalists. It is like adding fuel to the fire while bemoaning its evil effects."* If Mr. Havell is in the secret of any discovery that will destroy western capitalism and revolutionise modern industry, I would ask him to make it public. It would be very welcome news to all Asiatics.

Mr. Havell is a cautious prophet. He predicts that the "discovery of the artistic application of mechanical Science" which will sweep away the gigantic mills and factories of the West will be made within "a few decades." If we have to wait "a few decades" for the discovery, and in the meantime do the best we can with our old-world industries, our situation will, I am afraid, be infinitely worse than it now is. "A few decades" only have sufficed to convert India from the position of an exporter of cotton manufactures to a large importer of the same manufactures and have brought our once flourishing iron and copper industry to the verge of extinction. If what is being done now for the handloom industry were done fifty years ago, before foreign imports had attained the volume they

* *An Eastern View of Western Progress*, by "Asiaticus," (W. Newman & Co.), p. 8.

have, matters might have been different. But, at present, it would be as idle to expect it *alone* to effectually stem the tide of foreign imports, as it would be to expect a wall of mud to dam a river in flood. All we can reasonably expect from it now is to enable our weavers to hold their own, but not to recover much, if any, of the ground they have lost.

Among the causes which have been operating against the interests of the handloom-weaving as, indeed, of various other industries conducted on primitive methods, such as iron-smelting, copper-smelting, &c., the railway is probably the most important. Railways have no doubt done a deal of good. But by facilitating the transport of foreign manufactures, and by spreading "civilisation" which often means little else besides a taste for the showy trinkets and fineries of the West, they are to a large extent responsible for the decadence or extinction of these industries. It would probably be no exaggeration to say, that the railway whistle sounds the death-knell of such industries. As there is no likelihood of any decrease of railway extension in the near future, it will continue to exert its adverse influence, and will tend to add to the keenness of the competition between handmade and machine-made articles. Equipped with improved handlooms, our weavers may be able to maintain their ground, but more cannot be reasonably expected. They belong to one of the most ignorant and, therefore, one of the most conservative sections of our community. They are supposed to number 2,700,000. If it were possible to induce even a quarter of that number to adopt the improved handloom at once or even within two or three years, foreign imports might at least be partially driven out of the markets now held by them. But I have seen them and talked with them in various parts of India, and I have little hesitation in saying, that such a thing could be compassed only by a miracle. They, like the mass of our people, are born philosophers. They resign themselves to the will of the Providence, and they bear calamities with a patience and fortitude which would have done the heart of Epictetus good to see. They do not think of the morrow, and consequently have not that desire for the accumulation of wealth, which impels the occidental to hard, steady work. By the time a respectable number of our weavers have been taught the use of the improved handloom, and *persuaded* to take to it, the competition with machine-made articles will have become more acute, because while they have been learning, discussing and procrastinating, newly-constructed railways have been extending the domain of foreign produce. The benevolent chief of the Mourbhanj State has been trying to introduce the improved handloom among its weavers for more than a year now, but the result so far is far from encouraging. Persistent effort will no doubt meet with success; but before it is achieved, the railway will have tapped the State more effectively than it does now, and will have afforded the mill produce a footing from which it would be difficult to dislodge it. In this connection it is highly desirable that detailed reports of all experiments which are being tried now in the different parts of India for the improvement and expansion of the handloom industry be communicated to the next Industrial Conference which, I trust, will be an annual institution.

The extreme poverty of our weavers, as indeed that of the average peasantry, is a great handicap. I do not exactly know what the lowest price is at which the improved handloom could be supplied. But, it is not likely to be much less than twenty rupees, a sum which not many of our weavers can spare for investment. If even a quarter of our weavers had to be supplied with the improved loom, a capital of not less than thirteen crores and a half would be required. Notwithstanding the great enthusiasm which the swadeshi movement has happily evoked all over the country, I doubt if even a tenth portion of that capital could be raised within a decade. Because, it must be remembered, that the patriotic spirit is strongest only among the educated middle classes, as indeed, it is expected to be; and they are, as a rule, not overburdened with the good things of the world.

The caste-system is also in the way to some extent. The manufacture of cloth, like the smelting of iron—the two articles which are in universal demand throughout the country—is relegated to one of the lowest castes in the Hindu social system. The higher caste people who are usually more intelligent, more resourceful and less poor, generally consider the occupation of weaving as degrading. Some of our educated young men may rise superior to caste-prejudices and adopt it in preference to the drudgery and debasement of such service as is usually within their reach. But their number is not likely to be large. So the sphere of operations of those who devote themselves to the development of the handloom industry is pratically confined to the weaving castes, who being among the lowest are illiterate, ignorant, and adverse to innovation and to hard and steady work, except near large towns. They quite understand and appreciate religious teaching. Prophets like Kabir have found large numbers of followers among them.

But it takes them time to appreciate altruistic efforts to secure their happiness through temporal means. If you go into the interior and offer to teach them the use of the improved handloom, ten to one they will suspect that you have some selfish motive in doing so, and it would take some time to disabuse their minds of such suspicions.

It should be borne in mind that the days of mechanical invention are not yet over; and it is quite within the range of probability, that some discovery may be made within the next decade which will reduce the present cost of production of the mills, and thus enable them to steal a march over the handloom and intensify its struggle for existence.

The foregoing considerations will, I venture to think, make it abundantly clear, that handloom alone cannot be reasonably expected to drive the foreign produce from our markets, or even to make a very serious impression upon it. Let every step that it is possible to take be taken to secure the development of the handloom industry. But, at the same time, there should be no abatement of the efforts which are being made for the expansion of the mill-industry. I am fully alive to the evils wrought by labour-saving machinery. It fact some of the great inventions of modern Science which are considered by western writers as its chief title to commendation are, to my mind, its chief title to condemnation. But the Asiatics must either suffer themselves to be exploited and to be gradually reduced to a condition of extreme poverty, if not of national slavery, or adopt the industrial methods of the West with their concomitant evils which, however, I am happy to say, are never likely to be so serious in the East as they are in the West. Besides, when by establishing mills and factories on a large scale, the Asiatics are able to drive the foreign manufactures from their markets, the occupation of the Western capitalists will be gone to a great extent, and Europe will then revert, at least partially, to the happy old times of the "Cottage industry." That is a more likely contingency than the overthrow of occidental capitalism by the artistic development of modern Science as contemplated by philanthropists like Mr. Havell.

CHAPTER V

TECHNICAL AND SCIENTIFIC EDUCATION IN BENGAL

Pamphlet, 1886

TECHNICAL Education may be roughly defined to be training required for the Industries.* These are divisible into—

A. Industries dependent upon Science, or *Science-Industries*, such as, dyeing, tanning, sugar-refining, soap-making, glass-manufacture, electro-engineering, mining &c.

B. Industries which have a very remote, if any, connection with Science and which may be called *Art-Industries* such as engraving, modelling, carpentry, shoe-making, &c.

* Technical education may admit of a wider definition, so as to cover Legal and Medical Education, Agriculture &c. Here, however, the expression is used in its ordinary, restricted sense.

2. By slightly enlarging the scope of the existing Metropolitan Art School, and with suitable improvements and alterations in its machinery, the requirements of the training necessary for those who intend to follow the industries falling under the division (B) may be adequately met; and if necessary, classes for these industries may without any serious increase of expenditure be established in connection with the Primary and Middle Schools.

3. The case is far otherwise with the Science-Industries. Those who intend to prosecute them successfully must go through, first a general course of scientific training, and then a special course of instruction in the subject chosen for technical study. But until lately the education in our colleges (leaving out of course the strictly professional institutions, the Engineering and Medical Colleges) was of a purely literary character. The study of Science, it is true, has now been introduced, but in the words of Mr. Pedler, Professor of chemistry at the Presidency College, "in a theoretical and unsatisfactory manner." The arrangements for the teaching of Natural Science in our colleges are as a rule far from satisfactory. We have heard of a Calcutta college where one ordinary sized glass-caseful of apparatus and chemicals is considered

sufficient for the teaching of Chemistry and Physics. Yet the college is well known to be a very successful one; that is to say, it passes a large number of candidates for the University Examinations every year. The Calcutta University is primarily responsible for this highly unsatisfactory state of things. It takes cognisance of theoretical knowledge only, ignoring most lamentably the principle now universally recognised that practical tests should form the distinctive feature of Science Examinations. As a necessary consequence there prevails a vast deal of what is known as *cram.*

4. The first step, then, requisite for technical training in the Science-Industries is to introduce better methods of Science teaching in our colleges.* This could, I believe, be done most effectively by the Calcutta University following its London model more closely than it has done hitherto. We do not think it would be at all desirable to introduce Elementary Science in the Entrance Examination *at the sacrifice* either of

* The writer of the Home Department note on Technical Education justly observes :—

"As Science is the foundation of every branch of technical instruction the principles of Science ought to underlie the education of those whose aim in life is the practice of the Industrial Arts." para 76.

English or of the second language. Nevertheless, we fully agree with the writer of the Home Department Note on Technical Education and other authorities, that elementary science should be introduced in the High and Middle Schools ; and, just by way of encouragement, we would propose that the Elements of Physics and Chemistry be prescribed as *optional* subjects for the Entrance Examination, the marks obtained in them counting only towards the place of the candidates taking them up in the general list. Or, only one paper may be set in History and Geography, (Physical Geography being excluded altogether) instead of two as at present, and Elementary Science made *compulsory* by setting a paper in it. The object of the Entrance Examination should be to lay the foundation for general culture ; and it would, we think, be a distinct disadvantage to introduce specialism at so early a stage. However, the question as to how science could be most effectively ingrafted on the curriculum of the schools is one which is incapable of satisfactory settlement without thorough discussion ; and the proposals I have just made must be taken as mere suggestions put forward to invite discussion.

5. Whatever objections may be raised with respect to any attempt to introduce science in the Entrance

Examination, we are aware of none, at least of a very serious nature, to its introduction into the First Arts as an *alternative* branch of study except the general difficulty of getting competent teachers for all the subjects— a difficulty which will be taken into consideration presently. The students after passing the Entrance Examination, should decide upon their future career. For those who intend to pursue literature the present First Arts course will serve with perhaps some slight alterations. The rest may be grouped under three heads as follows :—

(A) Students for general science and its application to the Industries.

(B) Students for Engineering.

(C) Students for Medicine.

In each of these cases the Second Language, History and Logic may be altogether dispensed with, and the following alternative First Arts Course substituted for students coming under the heads (A) and (B).

(*a*) English	Two papers		
(*b*) Mathematics... ...	Do.		As at present.
(*c*) Physics...	Do.		

[Drawing [being intended for the Engineering, and Biology for the other students].

(*d*) Chemistry ... ... One paper

(*e*) Biology or Drawing Do.

For Medical Students Mathematics beyond the stage required for the Entrance Examination is not essential, and the following course may be found advantageous :—

(*a*) English ... ... Two papers.

(*b*) Botany ... ... Do.

(*c*) Zoology ... ... Do.

(*d*) Chemistry(Including Elementary Physics) Do.

So long as English remains the vehicle of instruction in our colleges, a knowledge of that language in indispensable and cannot be safely omitted from the Science Examination corresponding to the First Arts (the First Science Examination or whatever other name it may go by). It is obvious, however, that the English course needed for the Science students should be different from what is wanted for the Art students. All that is required of the former is sufficient knowledge to enable them to understand English scientific books and to express their ideas in English. The English Course, and the University Examination therein intended for them should be adjusted accordingly.

6. The fact of the University First Arts Examination being held at a rather large number of places*

* The number is 29 at present (1886).

precludes the possibility of the application of satisfactory practical tests at the Science Examinations. It is, therefore, highly desirable that the number of the F. A. Examination centres, at least for the Science Candidates, should be largely reduced. Indeed as the introduction of Science on the scale contemplated here is not likely to be effected in the near future any where except in the metropolis and two or three of the more highly advanced mofussil colleges, the holding of the First Science Examination at the metropolis only would not practically lead to any serious hardship.

7. After passing the First Science Examination, the students of general and technical Science should take up their special subjects of study. The present Science (B) course for the University degree ought to be considerably modified. The Science Students should not be called upon to pass in the English course; nor is it necessary, that Mathematics higher than the First Arts standard* should be made compulsory for them all. To illustrate by an example: For students desirous of making Physics or Chemistry their speciality it would be of very little use to make a critical study of the plays

*The First Arts Mathematical Course should, however be altered, so as to include Statics and Dynamics, as I believe it did, not long ago.

of Shakespeare, the poems of Milton or Wordsworth, or of any of the works of Burke, Pattison or De Quincey. All the branches of Natural Science have grown so largely of late, that it is impossible for any man to be equally proficient even in all the subdivisions of any one branch of Science. Zoology, for instance, has made such rapid progress within recent years, that a zoologist is now obliged to devote almost his exclusive attention to one class or order or even a family out of numbers of classes or orders or families into which the Animal Kingdom is divided. Such dispersion of energies as is fostered by the Calcutta University, is quite inconsistent with the spirit of the age. It cannot lead to any good result, at any rate, any result commensurate with the time, labour and energy spent. The Calcutta University appears to be tremendously behind the age, and it is high time the eyes of that body were opened.

8. The Entrance Examination lays the foundation for general culture. At the First Arts a step is taken towards specialism which should be further developed at the Science Examination corresponding to the B.A. Examination. In order to do this the (B) or Science course of this Examination should consist of the following subjects arranged in groups of two or three, the

candidates being required to take up any *one* of such groups :—

I. Pure Mathematics.
II. Mixed Mathematics.
III. Experimental Physics.
IV. Chemistry.
V. Botany.
VI. Zoology.
VII. Physiology.
VIII. Geology.
IX. Mental and Moral Science.

Mathematics (Pure and Mixed) with Experimental Physics may form one group ; Experimental Physics and Chemistry, another group : and so on. It need hardly be remarked, that the standard of proficiency required in each subject should be very high. Above all, a *practical examination should be held in every subject that admits of it.*

Both at the First Science Examination and at the degree Examination, candidates may take Honours in any subjects prescribed for the Pass Examinations.

9. If the reforms here suggested were carried out, a sound basis would be laid for Technical Education in the Science-Industries. It must not be understood, however, that those reforms are desirable in the interest of Technical Education only. They are urgently needed for the sake of a sound scientific education also. So that, apart from any consideration of the industrial application of Science, they will we trust, meet with

favourable consideration at the hands of our guardians of education.

10. It may be urged, not without some show of reason: What is the good of such High Scientific Education even for the Science-Industries? May we not benefit by the discoveries of the western Scientists? We may, but not without a thorough scientific training. To take a simple industry, say soap. The raw materials available for it here are not all the same as those used in Europe. For its manufacture on a commercial scale we must utilise *our raw materials*; it would never pay to import any of the principal ingredients from abroad. Caustic soda, for instance, may be made from some such substance as *saji*. And for this purpose, this substance has to be analysed, its impurities ascertained, and the *most economical methods* of purification and the preparation of the caustic lye from it *discovered*. All this cannot be done except by a specialist in Chemistry. Similar remarks would apply *mutatis mutandis* to good many other industries.

11. What is needed for Technical Education is to select a few Industries which are most likely to lead to satisfactory economic results, and to impart special instruction with a view to their development. The majority of the Industries which may be expected to be

profitable, such as Glass, Soap, Candle and Paper manufactures, Dyeing and Tanning are based upon Chemistry. For the instruction necessary for these, a *well equipped* chemical laboratory is essential. In connection with it, as well as for such industries as Electro-Engineering, and Electro-Metallurgy &c. there should be a Physical Laboratory. Again, Mining is an Industry for which there is a fairly promising field in India and Burmah. The completion of the projected Bengal-Nagpur railway—and their completion is only a question of time—will bring the coal and other mineral resources of Western Bengal and the Central Provinces within easy access, and will thus stimulate their development. The Petroleum industry of Burma and Eastern India is capable of considerable expansion. For Mining, a knowledge of geology is necessary. For neither, however, is any expensive laboratory required, the practical work in both must be done in the field.

12. In order to encourage the Science graduates to undergo special training in the Industries, it would be desirable to found scholarships. Indeed, otherwise, it would be impossible for most of them to prosecute their studies. The poverty of our middle class which furnishes by far the largest number of the best gra-

duates is well-known ; and this circumstance is aggravated by the peculiar conditions of our society. There are not many who can wait the completion of their educational career ; still fewer could wait any length of time when it is over without depriving themselves, and what is of more serious consequence, a large number of helpless souls entirely dependant upon them, perhaps even of the barest necessaries of life. Leisurely research under such conditions is out of the question.

13. Besides the Sciencc Graduates, those who may be actually engaged in any of the Industries and others should be admitted into the classes and laboratories for technical instruction. Indeed, the restrictions to the admission of students should be as few as possible. Examinations should he held, and certificates or diplomas given by the professors. But the Examinations need not have any connection with the University. Indeed, if the University be found unwilling so to remodel its science courses and the examinations therein as would lead to science-teaching worthy of the name at our colleges, the Institution where the technical training in the Science-Industries is to be imparted, may well undertake the work of High General Scientific education also ; and its Science diploma would be

certainly more valued by the public than the degree of the Calcutta University obtained by candidates who take up the present mongrel course, which goes by the name of the B. course.

14. The next question is, what is to become of the men who have received technical education in the Science Industries ? The existing manufactories are not sufficiently numerous to absorb but a small fraction of them. To complete their training they should if possible serve a term of apprenticeship. The Government might offer a scholarship or two tenable in Europe for that purpose. The Agricultural Scholarships are going abegging ; and those scholarships might in alternate years be well devoted to the promotion of Industrial Education, if any European factories could be persuaded to admit Indian apprentices.

15. Government cannot be reasonably expected to utilise the men who have received technical training, except perhaps in a small way. All that Government may be expected to do is to patronise articles of Indian manufacture ; and that is the declared policy of the Supreme, as well as, the Local Governments. The work of Government will practically cease with training up the men. The further work of starting factories, or of working mines should be undertaken by us. With

a large variety of raw materials in abundance, and scientific men to properly utilise them, and with cheap labour, there are good many industries which with judicious management are bound to yield an adequate return. It will be the duty of the practical technologists to point out the openings for profitable investements, and capital even in such a poor country will be forthcoming. One or two successful enterprises will lead to others. That our countrymen are not slow to follow a venture when it is seen to be profitable is evidenced by the number of the Oil and Flour Mills in Calcutta and the suburbs. The struggle for infant industries in a country where protective duties in any shape cannot even be thought of must be very hard ; but we must be prepared for it, and endeavour to minimise its hardships as best as we can.

16. Some idea of the machinery required for High Technical Education must have been gleaned from what has been said above. It is now to be considered, how to set up the different parts of the machinery, so as to do the largest amount of work in the most economical manner possible. The peculiar circumstances of our country render economy a consideration of importance in any scheme. At the same time, however, efficiency must not be sacrificed to economy. The two

must be combined ; and we shall now consider how that could be best done.

17. There is no *one* existing Institution which without *considerable expansion* involing *very heavy outlay*, could hold that place with regard to all the Science-Industries which the central Art School with but little enlargement of its scope and at a moderate additional cost to Government may do with respect to the Art-Industries. The able writer of the Home Department note on Technical Education is not unaware of this, as the following passage will show* :—

"For the schools which should fall under division A [the Science-Industries] no Central Institution at present in existence may serve all the purposes of control and direction ; but the Engineering Colleges will, at all events, serve the purpose to some extent."

In the Bengal Engineering College at Shibpore the teaching of Chemistry, Physics, Geology, Metallurgy and Mining, on which the Science-Industries are dependent is subservient to the requirements of a Civil Engineer, and is of a highly elementary character. *All of these subjects* are there taught by one and the same teacher— an arrangement of questionable efficiency even as regards the requirements of an ordinary Engineer. For

* *Op. cit.* Para 87.

the successful industrial application of the Sciences, however, the instruction must be *far more* advanced. The Chemistry needed for the Chemical Industries, for instance, must comprise both its Organic and Inorganic branches; and, above all, the instruction must be of a *highly practical* nature such as could be given by a specialist in chemistry with a well-appointed laboratory at his disposal. Similarly with the industries based upon Physics, Geology, Mining and Metallurgy.

18. We think the Science Department of the Presidency College would with some expansion serve the purposes of a central technological Institute for some of the most important industries *far better than the Engineering College.* At this institution there are, we believe, good Chemical and Physical Laboratories; and from what has been said before it will be abundantly apparent, that Chemistry and Physics, especially the former are the two Industrial sciences *par excellence.* On the other hand, at the Shibpore College, there are germs for the dovelopment of the Industries based upon Geology, Mining, and Metallurgy.

19. We have thus at the Presidency and Shibpore Colleges all the elements which are essential for the construction of a central Technological Institute. What is necessary is to work them up into a harmonious

whole. In doing this we have to keep in view not only the requirements of Industrial Instruction but also of Engineering, and Scientific Education. If the suggestions we have put forward above about the alternative First Arts Examinations for Science, and Engineering students were adopted, our task would be considerably lightened.

The location of the central Science and Technological Institute (which is the name we shall give to the institution we are attempting to construct) is a matter of convenience which it will be for the Educational authorities and Government to consider. There is nothing to hinder its being under the same roof as the Presidency or Engineering College except want of accomodation. If the proposed Institute be located elsewhere than the Engineering College it would probably be impracticable to avail ourselves of the services of the Professor who now teaches Geology, Mining, and Metallurgy at that College; so that two or three new men would be required to take charge of these subjects.

* * *

22. The Science and Technological Institute with proper arrangements, the details of which are susceptible of easy settlement, could be made to impart—

1. Preliminary instruction in Science to Medical, Engineering, and Science Students.

2. Advanced instruction in Natural Science to candidates either for the Science degrees of the University corresponding to B. A. and M. A., or for some Science diploma to be given by the proposed Institute.

3. Technical instruction in Industries dependent on Science.

4. Agricultural instruction.

We fully expect that the centralisation here suggested would be conducive to economy without being injurious to efficiency in the least degree.

23. The affiliation of the Science and Technological Institute with the Calcutta University will be necessary as it is to train up candidates for the proposed alternative First Arts Examinations intended for Medical, Engineering and Science Students, and for the degree Examinations in Science. But *the University need have no concern with the Technical Examinations. The central Institute should undoubtedly have sufficient prestige to make its diplomas and certificates valued by the public.*

24. We have throughout relied upon Government to take up the whole work of Technical Education. From what has been said above, the reason will be obvious. Several important constituents of the machi-

nery required for Technical Education are now working under Government management, direct or indirect. All that is needed is to bring them together at one place, make a few additions and alterations and set up the whole thing dexterously. So that highly expensive as the scheme we have put forward may appear, Government could in reality, work it out at but comparatively little extra cost. For any other agency, the whole thing would have to be organized almost afresh, and that would make it too expensive to be within the scope of any fund raiseable by subscription. Two movements were started a few years ago, one with the sole object of Technical education, and the other having this for one of its objects. The first, called the Indian League, has been a signal failure. The second, the Indian Association for the Cultivation of Science, has been doing *good work as far as its funds would allow.* But the funds at its disposal would not go far towards meeting the wants of Technical Education.

25. Even if the Government were to undertake the entire work of Technical Education, a great deal would still be left for the public to do. Beyond the stage of Laboratory or Field instruction, all that Government may be reasonably expected to do would be to foster

any industries that may be started. In order to help in the starting and development of Indian Industries, to point out to Government where and in what way its patronage or legislation may be advantageous, and to watch the cause of Technical Education generally, we think an organization is needed, which may be called the "Society for the Development of Indian Industries." Enormous difficulties may be expected to attend the early stages of Technical Education in this country; and the public must move earnestly and energetically to remove them. Whatever scheme of Technical Education may be adopted by Government, success would be impossible without the hearty co-operation of the public.

CHAPTER VI

SCIENTIFIC AND TECHNICAL EDUCATION IN BENGAL

(*The Statesman, July, 1906*)

IT is now twenty years since I first ventured to make some suggestions for the development of the scientific and higer technical education on this side of India ;* and it may be both interesting and profitable to take stock of the progress made within that period.

The Calcutta University exercises, through its examinations, a potent influence on the education of the province, and I shall first review the steps taken by it to promote scientific education. The first outward sign of the recognition by that body of the different branches of Natural Science as independent subjects of education was the institution of a science degree during the closing decade of the last century. But, the students

* "Technical and Scientific Education in Bengal."—1886.

going up for that degree have hitherto had no special preliminary preparation. Their curriculum after passing the Entrance Examination has been that of the First Examination in Arts which, as the name implies, is specially intended to meet the requirements of Arts students. The B. Sc. course was a sort of compromise between the literary and the scientific courses, and, like many such compromises, has to a great extent proved a failure. As I observed in my pamphlet on "Scientific and Technical education in Bengal;" whatever objections may be raised with respect to any attempt to introduce science in the Entrance Examination, we are aware of none, at least of a serious nature, to its introduction into the First Arts as an *alternative* branch of study. The students after passing the Entrance Examination should decide upon their future career. For those who intend to pursue literature, the present First Arts course will serve with perhaps slight alterations. The rest may be grouped under three heads :

(A) Students of General Science.

[The various branches of Natural Science.]

(B) Students for Engineering.

(C) Students for Medicine."

In each of these three cases, the second language,

history and logic may be altogether dispensed with and the following alternative course substituted for students coming under the heads (A) and (B).

(*a*) English—Two papers.

(*b*) Mathematics—Two papers.

(*c*) Physics—Two papers.

(*d*) Chemistry—One paper.

(*e*) Biology or drawing—One paper."

(Drawing being intended for engineering and biology for the other students.)

It is only since last year, that the Calcutta University has waked up to a sense of the necessity of early specialisation in modern scientific study, and I am glad to note that an Indermediate Science Examination (corresponding to the First Examination in arts) is about to be instituted for the special benefit of the science students. It differs from the one recommended by me twenty years ago in having three, instead of two papers in English and in omitting biology altogether. English being the medium of instruction in this country, a good knowledge of that language is no doubt indispensable. But I am still of opinion that two properly set papers should be quite enough to test it, and that all students of natural science, whatever may be the special subject taken up by them, should have a knowledge of elementary biology as they should have of chemistry and physics.

It is satisfactory to note, that there has been a marked improvement in the teaching of chemistry and physics at the Government colleges, especially at the Presidency College, where the physical and chemical laboratories have undergone considerable expansion. But the observations which I made in the eighties with regard to the inadequate arrangements for science teaching in the colleges affiliated to the Calcutta University unfortunately still hold good to a large extent. It would be hardly credited outside India, that in the beginning of the twentieth century, in the premier Government college in the metropolis of British India, the second city of the British Empire, there is no chair either for Botany or for Zoology. The only College in Bengal where there are chairs in those subjects is the Medical College of Calcutta, where they are taught in a most general way to meet the bare requirements of medical students, forty lectures in Zoology and twenty in Botany being considered sufficient for their purpose. It is true a chair in Biology has been recently established at the Presidency College. But the occupant of that chair has to lecture on Botany and Physiology, either of which subjects is large and important enough for the appointment of a specialist as Professor. A lectureship in Geology (including Mineralogy) has been established at the Presidency College during the period under review, but only as an appanage of the Geological Survey of India. It has been occupied by some seven officers of that department, that is, for about two years in the average by each of them. The greater portion of their time has necessarily been taken up by the work of the Survey, and it is only for four months during their recess time (from July to October) that they have been able to devote three or four hours a week to their professorial duties at the Presidency College. Geology has grown so largely of late that even a whole-time man, however able, could do but scant justice to all its branches. For effective teaching it is desirable to have a specialist Professor for each of its three main branches—Geology proper, Mineralogy and Palæontology. One can easily imagine, therefore, what progress might be expected from the intermittent lectures of a Professor changed every two years, who had to be away from Calcutta for the greater portion of the year, who could remain there only during the hottest and unhealthiest part of the year when strenuous brain work is not practicable, and who even then had to perform his professorial duties during leisure hours snatched from the work of a department by which he is employed as a permanent whole-time officer. When I had the honour of occupying the chair of Geology at the Presidency College (1901 to 1903) I drew the attention of the educational authorities to this unsatisfactory state of things, and had a laboratory assistant appointed not without some difficulty. But even with his help, I found I could do but little justice to the duties of my post. I must say, matters have improved since my retirement, in that the present occupant of the geological chair is an officer of the Geological Survey who is stationed in Calcutta throughout the year.

Though the record of the progress of scientific education which the Calcutta University and the colleges affiliated to it has to show for the last two decades is not so satisfactory as it might well have been, the future is fraught with promises and possibilities which, it is boped, will be at least partially realised. The Calcutta University will, under the new Act exercise a greater control over the education of the Province than it has done hitherto ; and that control may be productive of good as well as of evil depending upon the way in which it is exercised. Research scholarships in science have been recently instituted by Government ; an agricultural college and research institute are about to be started at Pusa ; the Tata Research Institute, the establishment of which is not likely to be deferred much longer, is expected to exercise a very wholesome influence upon the scientific education of the country; and the Forest School at Dehra Dun promises to become an important centre of scientific research. I have, however, in this connection to repeat the remarks which I made ten years ago in my "History of Hindu Civilisation under the British Rule:" "Scientific education offers openings in Europe which may as yet be said to be almost absent in India, at least for the Indians. Scientific research is liberally endowed in Europe, so that specialists may devote themselves to their favorite subjects with their animal wants fairly supplied; and there are influential societies which watch over their interests. In India there are under the Government a few small departments which are maintained chiefly for scientific research, and a few larger departments for which a scientific training is necessary. Both these classes of departments are almost exclusively officered by Europeans; with regard to the departments for scientific research, it is sometimes argued, as if, as Orientals, the Hindus were incapable of it whatever their education might be. It is true, the ancestors of the Modern Hindus had made but little progress in natural science, but the ancestors of the modern Europeans had not made any better progress. Modern Natural Science does not date back earlier than the middle of last century. The Hindus successfully cultivated astronomy, which requires observational powers of no mean order. They also made valuable observations on plants and minerals. In their conceptions of the duration and mutability of our planet; of the gradual evolution of the organic world; of an ethereal substance, infinite and eternal; of material substance as aggregates of atoms; and of light and heat as different forms of the same substance, they had anticipated some of the fundamental principles of modern science. The facts, that they have done this in the past, that they have made some contributions to science, however humble, in the present, that an Oriental nation like the Japanese has, within so short a space of time as a decade or two, risen to scientific eminence, show that the mere fact of his being an Oriental does not argue an inborn capacity for scientific research in the Hindu. A civilised Government has certain well recognised responsibilities towards its subjects, one of which is to spend the revenue derived by taxing them upon objects which are calculated to conduce, at least principally, to their good. We see no reason why with an improved system of scientific education, and, with just and sympathetic treatment of the young men trained in science, they will not be able to take that place in modern scientific world which they may be expected to do under the rule of one of the foremost nations of the world. The reason of the recent success of the Japanese in the field of science is that their young men, trained under western scientists, instead of being thwarted, discouraged, and set down as incapable, have been aided, encouraged, and stimulated by their Government to pursue science."*

In regard to higher technical education, progress during the last two decades has, I regret to say, been practically nil in Bengal. A Technical Institute worthy of the name is as much a desideratum now as it was twenty years ago. Some so-called technical schools have been established within the period; but the teaching imparted in them is almost exclusively confined to surveying, carpentry and black-smith's work and is not culculated to enable the alumni to take any part in the development of the resources of their country. Within the period under review manganese mining has been started and developed to the status of an important industry, the expansion of the coal, petroleum and jute

* O cit. Vol. III., pp. 96—99.

industries has gone on steadily, and in the case of the mining industries by leaps and bounds. But all this has been effected almost exclusively by Western capital and Western enterprises.

Coal mining is probably the principal industry of Bengal. But hitherto there has been no arrangement for the proper teaching of mining in any institution in Bengal. It is only during the present year that a class in mining has been opened at the Engineering College at Shibpore. There is a large field for metal lurgy in India, but I am not aware of any institution in this country which gives any training in that subject. A Commission appointed five years ago to recommend measures for the furtherance of technical education suggested the establishment of six institutes of industrial experiment and instruction at an approximate capital and annual cost of Rs. 3,30,000, and Rs. 1,87,000 respectively—institutes of texile, metal pottery and china-ware, sericulture, and tanning industries. Not one of them has come into existence, though four years have elapsed since the submission of the report of the Industrial Commission.

I must observe that the blame for this sad neglect of technical education in the past does not rest on Government alone. If my compatriots of Bengal were as fully convinced of the paramount necessity of such education as our brethren of the Western Presidency, they might ere now have at least had an institution like the Victoria Jubilee Technical Institute of Bombay. A sum of over two lakhs of rupees raised to found a permanent memorial in honour of Lord Ripon formed the nucleus of the fund with which that institute was established. Similar funds have within the past twenty years been also raised in Bengal; but there has been wanting the earnest desire to apply them for such a purpose of obvious utility as technical education instead of squandering them away on ill-considered schemes which do but little good to the country or on empty and unsubstantial show and pageantry.

The future, however, in the case of technical, as in that of scientific education, appears to be hopeful. The Government of India instituted two years ago scholarships for the technical training of students in Europe. The Government of Bengal has just pledged its word to develop the local Engineering College into a technical institute of the first order. An association recently established in Calcutta has during the last two years been awarding scholarship to students for technical training in Europe, America and Japan. Another association just established is about to start a technical institute,* the first of the kind in Calcutta. Technical education will also, I am informed, be undertaken by a third association, the National Council of Education, and another body of patriotic gentlemen raised a few months ago a fund, called the National Fund, which, I understand, is going to be devoted mainly to the imparting of education in weaving.

It should be noted, however, that while the collection of so many separate funds just mentioned for technical education within the last six months, is certainly an index of the awakening of Bengal to the gravity of her industrial situation, and, to that extent, an augury of future good, it hardly betokens the full development of the qualifications necessary to grapple with it successfully. The various funds at present available for technical education in Bengal do not, I find, amount altogether to more than ten lakhs of rupees—a sum which is hardly sufficient even for a modest institute like the Victoria Jubilee Technical Institute of Bombay or the Kalabhavan of Baroda; and I need hardly point out, that one well-equipped technical institute is likely to accomplish far more solid work than two or three badly equipped ones.

* This institute has now been established under the name of the Bengal Technical Institute. (Aug. 1906).

SECTION II

HISTORICAL

CHAPTER I

CASTE SYSTEM IN INDIA: ITS ORIGIN AND HISTORY

(Lecture delivered at the Bristol Museum and Library, March 1880)

THE caste-system, as you are no doubt aware is one of the most characteristic features of the social structure of the Hindus, who constitute about two-thirds of the vast population of India. Caste-regulations govern the life of a Hindu from the moment of his birth to that of his death. His religion is so intimately connected with caste that it is very difficult to say where the one begins and the other ends. Disregard of the ordinances of caste is not only a social crime but a religious heresy. In fact, it would, perhaps, be no exaggeration to say, that with a large class of the Hindus, religion is practically nothing else but the rigid observance of a series of caste rules and regulations.

I shall have to point out to you some of the characteristics of the caste-system now existing in India later on; but I shall not take up your time with descriptive details, which you could gather from several more or less trustworthy accounts published in the English language. Nor is it my object to dwell at length on the influence which caste has had on the social evolution of the Hindus. I propose this evening to trace the origin and narrate the history of this celebrated, but as yet imperfectly understood, institution. In these days of scientific progress such an inquiry must no doubt be one of great theoretical interest. I need hardly remind you that it is consistent explanation and not bare description that constitutes science; and that this is true for natural, as for social, science—a science which notwithstanding the immense and peculiar difficulties it has to contend with, will probably at no distant day rank very high in our estimation. I think it necessary to remark at the outset that the interest of our subject is not solely, or even mainly, theoretical; it is highly important also from a practical point of view.

At the very threshold of our subject, a question naturally present itself—what is caste? It would be perhaps hopeless to attempt to define a word the vagueness of which has been established by such long use in modern literature, and that too by authors of established reputation. We shall, however, consider the question together when we have before us the facts that are necessary for its determination.

The hypotheses which have been proposed to account for the origin of caste may be conveniently classed under three heads :—

I.—Those which ascribe to it a transcendental origin. They are embodied in the speculations of Indian authors since the period during which the hymns of the Rigveda were composed. It would be impossible, and, I may also say, unnecessary, to state them all, much less criticise or examine them in detail within the limited time at my command. Those who are curious will find them carefully collected in the first volume of Dr. Muir's very valuable work entitled "Original Sanscrit Texts." I shall content myself with remarking generally that they are far from being strictly uniform or rigidly consistent. But I cannot pass by without briefly noticing one of them, which claims our attention on the ground of its being the most widely adopted, and, perhaps, as far as the hypothesis is concerned, the simplest and most congruous of all. Stated in a few words, it amounts to this: that the four original castes, *viz.*, Brahmanas, Kshatriyas,

Vais'yas, and S'udras, sprung from the mouth, arms, thighs, and feet of the creator respectively; and that all the other castes—and there are hundreds of them—arose from these four by intermarriage or degradation, or both.

The first part of this hypothesis is evidently derived from an allegory, which is certainly not so ancient as the greatest majority of the hymns of the Rigveda.* That allegory describes, not inappropriately, the Brahmans who were chiefly teachers and instructors at the time when it was composed, not as originated from, but as being the mouth of Purusha; the Kshatriyas who were the warriors of that time, as his arms, that is, the *seat of strength;* and the Vais'yas who formed the mass of the population—agriculturists, artisans, &c., as the lower parts of his body. The facts which I shall lay before you will make it clear, that in the earliest period of Indian History these three castes were not in existence; that they were slowly separated out of the original Aryan community; and that the fourth caste, the Sudra, a term which occurs only once in the whole collection of the Rigveda, and that too in one of the undoubtedly latest hymns—was not established till

* This allegory is contained in the Purusha Sukta of the Rigveda.

towards the close of the Rigvedic period. Thus, the first part of the hypothesis which explains the origin of the four primitive castes by supposing them to be coeval with creation will be completely refuted.

The second part, which derives all the remaining castes by intermarriage and degradation, is equally fallacious. It is probable that some of the "mixed" castes were the result of intermarriage. But there can be no question that a great many of them, and almost all the so-called "fallen" or "degraded" castes mentioned in the Manusamhita, the highest authority on caste, were mere designations of nations, races and tribes, with whom the Aryans came in contact as they spread from their northwestern colony, and as their commerce, and intercourse with foreign nations increased. Our Indo-Aryan ancestors had unfortunately a great deal too much of a speculative turn of mind. They saw—as we do still more or less everywhere—that some are born to lead, others to be lead; some in wealth and influence, others in poverty and obscurity. It would not have been enough for them to have solved this problem historically—as the necessary consequence of social evolution. There would still be the great, and to them, the insuperable objection—why should there be such an unjust evolution? Why should the mere accident of one's birth affect his prospect so materially? They wanted to go to the very root of the matter; and they thought they had been successful when they propounded that from the very beginning of creation men were born to be of unequal social rank—such was the design of the creator himself. As in their speculations, and those of their brethren in ancient Europe, on cosmogony, the early Indian philosophers did not try so much to build theories on obsrved facts, as to make facts suit their pet theories. Starting with the hypothesis, that there were but four great classes at the creation—classes which composed the Indo-Aryan Society at the time when that hypothesis was proposed—they soon came to see that outside their territories, there were a great many peoples, some in the worst conditions of savagery, others nearly as high in the scale of civilisation as they themselves. In order to be consistent, they must connect these different races and tribes, however remotely, with the four original castes; for according to them, there was none else at the creation. Consequently, when, for instance, they came to know the Greeks and the Chinese they designated these nations as degraded Kshatriyas* —this high position being assigned, no doubt because they found these nations to be considerably advanced in

* Manu, X. 43-44.

civilisation. Later still, when the merchants of modern Europe went to India, the Hindu writers evolved out of their inner consciousness a fanciful pedigree for them, and made them out to be a " mixed" caste.*

II.—There is another class of hypothesis which, once in great favour but now all but discarded, differ from those I have just mentioned in ascribing the institution of caste to a man of genius a great legislator, instead of to a Divine Being. As the best known of this class, I shall take the one which has all the weight of authority due to its advocacy by James Mill. " So long as men roam" says Mill, "in the pastoral state, no division of classes or of labour is known. Every individual is a shepherd and every family provides for itself the commodities with which it is supplied. As soon as the cultivation of land which yields a more secure and plentiful subsistence, occupies a great share of the common attention, the inconvenience of this universal mixture of employments is speedily felt. The labours of the field are neglected, while the cultivator is engaged at the loom, or repelling the incursions of an enemy......................When the Hindus were lingering in this uneasy situation, it would appear that there arose among them one of those

* See *Jatimala*, &c.

7

superior men, who are capable of accelerating the improvement of society.

Perceiving the advantages which would accrue to his countrymen from a division of employments, he conceived the design of overcoming at once the obstacle by which this regulation was retarded ; and clothing himself with a divine character, established as a positive law, under the sanction of heaven, the classification of the people and distribution of occupations......Ignorant that professions when once separated, were in no danger of being confounded, he established a law which the circumstances of the time very naturally suggested, but which erected a barrier against further progress ; *that the children of those who were assigned to each of the classes, into which he distributed the people, should invariably follow the occupations of their father through all generations.*"*

I need not stop to point out the fallacies of this hypothesis which will be completey exposed to you as I proceed.

III.—The third and last class of hypotheses includes those that are based upon the actual facts in the history of the people of India. You are no doubt aware of some

* Mill's "History of British India," Vol. I.—(The italics are mine).

of the marvellous results which have followed the discovery of a language, sweeter and purer, and more ancient, than that of Greece, and of a literature on the whole quite as rich as the most ancient classical literature of Europe. One of those results is the tendency to fill up with well-authenticated facts the pages of the history of ancient India, which, half a century ago, if not quite blank, was all but a collection of tales and anecdotes. During that period, the indefatigable researches of Colebrooke, Wilson, Max Muller, Roth, Lassen, and a host of other distinguished scholars have brought to light a vast mass of the most valuable materials regarding the past condition of India. There has not yet been time to sort, arrange, and properly systematise these materials; and the hypotheses of caste based upon them are only indications of the method by which we could arrive at a correct explanation. But even as such, those hypotheses are far more valuable than all the most elaborate speculations of the ancient Indian writers put together. Some scholars have put forth weighty suggestions as to the manner in which caste originated, at first, three thousand years ago; and many more have recognised a general dissimilarity between the modern and the ancient caste of India. But no systematic attempt has been made as yet to point out the exact relation of the one to the other. In proposing to perfo.m this by no means easy task I do not pretend to any originality of research worth the name. But I have availed myself very largely of the materials I have just alluded to, and I cannot be sufficiently grateful to those great men, who by their deep devotion and unflinching perseverance have placed them within our reach.

In order that you might be able to follow me better, I have divided Indian History into five periods. The dates are only approximate and entirely provisonal.

1. Rigvedic Period ... (B. C., 2002-1400.)
2. Brahmanic Period .. (B. C., 1400-1000.)
3. Rationalistic Period ... (B. C., 1000- 300.)
4. 5. Buddhist Hindu and Hindu Period. } (B. C., 300, to the present time.

I.—RIGVEDIC PERIOD.—More than 4000 years have elapsed since a colony of Aryans from the Highlands of Central Asia, where they had lived together with your own ancestors, and the ancestors of the Greeks, Romans, and many other nations of Europe as members of one community, settled on the banks of the Indus and its tributaries. While still located in the Punjab and its vicinity, they were in the habit of singing hymns as prayers, or in praise or honor of their deities, and these hymns probably composed during a period of some 500 years, from B. C.

2000 to 1500, have been preserved in a most remarkable collection, now no doubt well known to you, at least by name—the Rigveda. The evidence afforded by this unquestionably the most ancient, and one of the most precious relics of Aryan history, shows beyond the shadow of a doubt that until towards the very close of the Rigvedic period, the Aryans were strangers to any kind of caste distinctions amongst themselves.* Any one who had the gift and the talent to compose a hymn which should attract the attention, and command the admiration of his brethren, was honoured with the appellation of 'Brahman,' that is, a Sage, an offerer of prayer. Any one who rose to distinction in the profession of arms was eulogised under the epithet of 'Kşhatriya'—that is, a man possessing power. † But 'Brahman' or 'Kshatriya', wise man, or powerful man, he was a 'vis, that is, one of the people.

* We do indeed, in certain texts, meet with such expressions as *panchakshitayah*, &c. But they cannot be interpreted to allude to the four *varnas* and the Nishadas, any more than to Gandharvas, Pitris, Devas, Asuras and Rákshasas. The very existence of these two interpretations of the terms, one advocated by such a high authority as Sayaṇácharya, and the other by no less a scholar than Yáska, would shew that they were mere suppositions put forward by Brahmanical writers long after the composition of the Vedic hymns.

† Muir's "Sanscrit Texts" ; Vol. I, p.p. 258, &c.

There are, however, indications in the Rigveda of a gradual differentiation of two very vaguely defined orders—the Bráhmanas and the Rájanyas or Kshatriyas, corresponding roughly to your clergy and nobility. The term Brahman, which in the earlier part of the Rigvedic period could be applied to any member of the Aryan community who offered up prayer or composed a striking devotional hymn, became restricted towards the latter part of that period to signify a kind of priest.* Later still, the descendants of these priests were, though in only a few passages, † distinguished under the appellation of "Bráhmanas"—a derivative word signifying the son of a Brahman. There is, however, nothing to shew that the Brahmanas as yet formed an exclusive order. From the extreme paucity of texts in which the word 'Kshatriya' is appropriated to the nobility, as well as from the all but entire absence of the term 'Rájanya' ‡

* 'Brahman' (m.) is evidently connected with 'Brahman' (n.), prayer. There were Vedic poets of regal origin, such as Trasadasyu, Devapi, &c. Even the offspring of a Dási, Kavasha Ailusha, was the author of several hymns.

† Out of 45 hymns in which the terms "Bráhmana" and "Brahman" occur the former is used in nine only. (Muir, *op. cit*, I.)

‡ This term "Rájanya" occurs only in the Purusha Sukta.

which is the alternative designation of that order, and which is related to 'Rájan,' a king, in the same way as 'Bráhmana' is to 'Brahman' in the sense of priest, we may safely infer that the Aryan princes and their relations had not yet come to be separated from the body of the people by anything like a clear line of demarcation. The name assigned to the third caste is 'Vis,' or its derivative 'Vaisya.' But throughout the Rigveda, except in one of the very latest hymns, (*viz*., the Purusha Sukta) the whole of the Aryan colony, kings, priests, and all, are included under the name 'vis,' people.

But, before the last notes of the last hymn were chanted by the last of the Rigvedic bards, his brethren had established a caste system—a system composed of two well-defined, exclusive, ethnological castes. Before the Aryans came to India, there had been several waves of immigration.* The Dravidians were the earliest race that entered India from north-west, and they found it already occupied by Kols, and other savage tribes whose descendants still live, fossilised as it were, in the hilly regions of Central and Eastern India. A fresh invasion of some Scythian races drove the Dravidians across the Vindhya hills to the forests of Southern

* Caldwell's "Comparative Grammar," pp. 108 ff.

India, the Deccan. As the Aryans spread eastward from the banks of the Indus, they came in collision with the Scythian aborigines, who, naturally enough, opposed their advance, fought them, disturbed their sacrifice, and harassed them in endless ways. For such acts, which no doubt seemed to the Aryans acts of doubtful courtesy, they called their adversaries, "Dasyus" ("robbers") ; "Rakshas" ("evil spirits,") &c. Epithets of the grossest invective were heaped on the devoted heads of the poor aborigines. They are described as irreligious, impious, and lowest of the low ; they are also in some texts contemptuously called *black-skinned*—a very significant epithet, as the Sanskrit term for 'Caste' primarily means colour, which would point to an original difference of colour as the first origin of caste. The Aryan immigrants, like the dominant races of ancient Peru and Egypt, had a fairer colour than the Scythian aborigines. Thus, during the Rigvedic period, there were, if I may so express myelf, two 'colors'—the fair (Aryan), and the black (Dasyuite or Dása). So long as these two classes were related to each other as belligerents there could be no question of caste. But the Aryans ultimately succeeded in conquering and subjugating their opponents ; and instead of exterminating the conquered tribes, or reducing them to a condition of slavery, they followed a policy characterised by mercy and humanity. The Aboriginal tribes—now called Sudras*—were incorporated with the Aryan society though on the hard condition, that they should occupy the lowest position in it.

Thus was formed a mixed society composed of two perfectly distinct ethnological castes. This union, and the subsequent mixture of the Aryans and non-Aryans, originally differing in many essential respects from each other, is the key to the most important phenomena in the history of ancient India. The numerical strength of the A ryas was probably vastly inferior to that of the aborigines ; but the intellectual and moral superiority of the former was in almost inverse ratio. They exerted the most enormous influence, not only on the northern Scythians, whom they mostly conquered, but also on the Dravidians of the south, amongst whom they settled on perfectly amicable terms, but who, nevertheless, tamely acknowledgd their supremacy, and voluntarily consented to occupy the social position assigned to them —no force acts so powerfuly on human mind as moral force.

* In the Atharvaveda, and the Samayacharika Sutras, the Aryas are not only contrasted with Dasas or Dasyus, but also with Sudras.

II. BRAHMANIC PERIOD.—As time rolled on, the hymns which the bards of olden times had sung became more and more antiquated. Our Aryan ancestors had great faith in them. Those hymns had led their forefathers to victory, and had brought down countless blessings from above. The art of writing had not yet been invented ; and the hymns were very numerous and very long. There were 1,017 of them ; and each would on the average, fill one page of an octavo volume. This was not all : every hymn must be recited in a particular manner—every word, every syllable must be pronounced in a prescribed way. Besides, many idioms of the majority of the hymns gradually became obsolete ; their language was, to the Sanscrit of the Brahmanic period, somewhat like what the English of Chaucer is to the English of the present day. All these circumstances tended to make the Brahmans more and more exclusive as an order. They treasured up the hymns in their memory, and officiated at the sacrifices. In a limited community like that of the Rigvedic period, of which agriculture was almost the sole occupation, any one who had ability and a poetical turn of mind could leave his work in the field for a little while to invoke the Muses. His composition would be communicated to the members of his community in a few days, and if it succeeded in becoming popular it would be remembered by them all for a long time, somewhat like a popular song in a large city, which one hears hummed, and whistled, and played wherever he goes. But times had changed. The Aryan territories now covered a considerably wider area; population had increased manyfold; and considerable progress was made in the arts and manufactures. Every Aryan was expected to have gone through the hymns once. But very few of those who were engaged in the ordinary occupations of life could afford space in their brains for 1,017 long hymns, with obsolete idioms and expressions, so as to be able to reproduce them at a given notice.

Picture to yourselves a thoroughly earnest semi-civilised Christian people, with unwritten Bible—a Bible, every line of which is handed down by tradition. Why, the men whose profession it should be to keep the whole of the Bible in their memory would be looked upon with peculiar awe and veneration; they would be regarded as mediators between heaven and earth; and unless they are altogether above the influence of human weaknesses and human passions, they would not fail to take advantage of the faith and credulity of the remainder of their community, and arrogate to themselves important privileges of an exclusive character,

Besides, being the sole depositaries of sacred knowledge. they would naturally bring up their sons to their profession, not only because they would prefer to do so, but also because qualification for the profession of priesthood under these circumstances would require a lifelong study.

The Second Class—The Kshatriyas or Rájanyas—composed of princes, their kinsmen and followers, became more and more specialised with the gradual extension of Aryan territories and the consequent increase in the number of petty principalities.

The mass of the Aryas formed the THIRD CLASS, the Vaisyas. During the earlier years of the Brahmanic Period, however, these three classes must have interlapped. But the complete subjugation of the aboriginal population worked an important change. Though they are generally described by their conquerors as utterly barbarous, there are passages in the Rigveda which shew that they were not devoid of the elements of civilisation. On their overthrow, their cattle, land, and all other resources were possessed or commanded by the dominant race. They were not indeed made slaves, but were reduced to a servile condition, and had probably at first to work for bare subsistence. They were forbidden to accumulate wealth, lest they should become insolent towards their superiors, and their property was theoretically held to belong to their masters Though there is satisfactory evidence that the severity of these injunctions was soon mitigated, and that they were perhaps never carried practically into effect, they show that the Sudras did not receive anything like an adequate share of the wealth which they were to no small extent instrumental in creating. Thus was caused a very unequal distribution of wealth in the Indian society. The higher classes, the original Aryas, or as they now styled themselves, *Dvijas*, "twice-born," especially the Brahmans and Kshatriyas, became rich at the expense of the poor Sudras. Inequality of social influence was the consequence of this inequality of wealth. Besides, the accumulation of wealth by the Dvijas furthered the division of labour amongst them, and afforded the Brahmanas opportunity for devoting themselves entirely to their pursuits. The Rigvedic poets belonged, as a rule, to the mass of the people. By far the greater number of their prayers were for cattle, grain, and similar earthly blessings—a fact which shews they had, like the rest of their community, to struggle for existence. They could not afford much time for speculation—their attention was all but engrossed by temporal objects. But now the Brahmanas obtained leisure for speculating upon theosophical and philosophical subjects, and for elaborating and thus complicating, the sacrificial rites and ceremonies of their ancestors. Consciously or unconsciously, they also enveloped these ritualistic ceremonies in so dark a mystery that none but professional adepts could properly interpret them. Thus the poetical nature-worship of the primitive Indo-Aryas stiffened into a dry creed of sacrifice and penance (Brahmanism.) Liturgical treatises, known as the *Brahmanas*, containing elaborate rules for the performance of sacrifices, were composed. The minutest rules were framed to make penance, not only for mistakes committed and observed during the performance of a sacrifice, but also for hypothetical omissions which might have slipped the observation of priests. Thus the liturgical literature became so very cumbersome, and the sacrificial ceremonial so very intricate, that the Kshatriyas and Vaisyas were obliged to leave them to the care of the Brahmanas, who were thus created sole trustees, as it were, of the religious welfare of the twice-born classes, and from the nature and importance of their function occupied the highest social rank.

Thus the Brahmanas came to form, though for a short period, a powerful sacerdotal hierarchy, and claimed for themselves several exclusive privileges. But the Brahmans, Kshatriyas and Vaisyas being differentiated out of the original Aryan community enjoyed many privileges in common, the most important of which were investiture with the sacred thread, the performance of sacrifice, and the study of the Scriptures. The Sudras, however, who formed the fourth and lowest caste, were, as we would expect from the circumstances of their admission into the Aryan society, excluded from all these privileges. The duty prescribed for them was to serve the three higher classes. The inborn Aryan pride of birth and spirit of aristocracy are reflected in the laws which were framed to keep the Sudra as distinct from these classes as possible. His condition, however, was much better than slavery. He could choose his own master. The law against his accumulation of wealth could not have been strictly carried out, as in the very book where that law occurs, it is stated that his property should on his death be shared by his children. His master could punish him only as he could punish his son or pupil. And, it is even enjoined that he is to be respected by the Dvijas in his old age.*

III. Rationalistic Period—It was not long before the ascendancy of the Brahmanas established during

* Manu II, 137.

the last period was disputed by the other classes of the Aryan society. The legends representing a Brahmana hero (Rama Jamadagnya) as having exterminated the Kshatriyas thrice seven times, and, subsequently, as himself vanquished by the Kshatriya Rama, the hero of the Ramayana, and a host of other legends, indicate in unmistakeable language the contests that went on between the Brahmanas and Kshatriyas after the establishment of Brahmanism. The complicated and elaborate sacrificial rites and ceremonies, which were the characteristic features of that religion, formed, as we have seen, the chief basis of Brahmanic influence. But, an important movement, in which the Kshatriyas seem to have taken the leading part, began in reaction against the exaggeration of the efficacy and importance of sacrifice, and terminated in the establishment of a sort of modified, rationalistic, Brahmanism. Such is the high notion entertained about sacrifices by the *Brahmanas* that according to one of these,* the gods themselves became immortal by repeated sacrifices.

At this period a class of works known as the *Upanishads* appeared, which put forth the doctrine of the superiority of spiritual knowledge to sacrificial

* *Satapatha Bráhmana*, X 4.3.9. See also Haug's *Aitareya, Bráhmana* i. pp. 8, 73 ff.

ceremonies. "It is the knowledge of the Supreme, Spirit" says one Upanishad, "that makes a man immortal."* "Those who imagine," says another, "that oblations and pious gifts are the highest object of man are fools; they do not know what is good." Men began to argue: "If a beast slain in a sacrifice will itself go to heaven, why then does not the sacrificer forthwith offer his own father? If beings in heaven are gratified by our offerings here, then why not give the food down below to those that are on the housetop?" The seed of rationalism sown by the Upanishads soon brought forth a rich harvest of earnest speculation. The field of enquiry gradually widened from cosmogony and theogony, to psychology, ethics and metaphysics; various schools of philosophy sprang up; and rationalistic treatises began to appear in great abundance.

The sacrifices which formed the essential doctrine of Brahmanism were of two kinds—(1) The grand and elaborate sacrifices,† in which the services of large number of priests were necessary; and (2) the simple domestic sacrifices consisting of the Five Sacraments or Devotional Acts, *viz.*, (i) an oblation to the gods offered on the domestic fires, (ii) an offering in honor of all sen-

* Brihad Aranyaka Upanishad IV. 4, 14.

† Asvala. Grihya Sutr, I.

tient beings, (iii) an offering to the Manes, (iv) repetition of the Vedas, and (v) gifts to men and hospitality.* With the progress of rationalism, the reactionary movement against Brahmanism, the first class of sacrifices gradually fell into desuetude.† These, however, were the only sacrifices at which the services of the Brahmans were essential. The Five Sacraments still continued to be performed by the twice-born classes ; but Brahmana, Kshatriya or Vaisya, he did not require the assistance of priests at these simple sacrifices. He was his own priest ; his home was his place of sacrifice ; and the materials he required for it were of the simplest character,—rice, clarified butter, water, and a log of wood. Thus the establishment of rationalistic Brahmanism struck at the root of Brahmanical ascendancy, by shaking mens' faith in the efficacy of those sacrifices on which were based their pretension to the religious trusteeship of the Dvijas, and by opening a path—the path of knowledge—which any Dvija seeking for salvation might follow independently, to reach the goal of his desires.

The Brahmans saw the danger of their situation. The priestly function had held them together as a class. But now they ceased to form a priesthood. Priestcraft

* Manu, iii. 68ff ; Asvala. Grihya, III. i.

†They are only incidentally mentioned in the Manusamhita.

came, in fact, to be held in all but utter contempt. They were no longer an order or corporation; their influence as a caste was at an end: they were, so to say, secularised. The gradual increase in their number also aided this important change. The Brahmans, however, wisely enough, were liberal and conciliatory towards their opponents. A philosopher, so long as he gave his consent, however nominal, to the authority of the srciptures, could teach and maintain his doctrines, howsoever heretical they might otherwise be. It did not matter much whether he believed in the existence of God or not. It would be quite enough if he did not openly deny the eternal infallibility of the Vedas. The Brahmans boldly engrafted the doctrines of the Upanishads and of the systems of philosophy to which these works gave birth upon Brahmanism itself. They still continued to exert very great influence. But it was not as a class that they did so; their influence came to be altogether personal, confined to the wise and learned amongst them. We have abundant evidence of this change in the Maunsamhita—the so-called "Institutes of Manu." It is there laid down, that an uneducated Brahmana is like a wooden horse, or an antelope made of leather—has nothing but the name.* Many of the

* Manu. II. 157.

privileges there claimed for the Brahmanas are claimed only for the wise and learned amongst them, not for them as a class. Thus it is said that no good whatsoever results from presents made to ignorant Brahmanas.* The right of keeping a treasure if found is not claimed for any Brahmana, but for learned Brahmanas only.† In the Manusamhita we read of many Brahmans who followed the occupations of the lower classes. There were Brahmanas who earned their living by selling meat, by low traffic, by dancing, by making bows and arrows, by taming elephants, horses, camels, and by tillage. There were Brahman shepherds, Brahman oilmen, and Brahman falconers.‡ The social position of such Brahmans could not have been far superior to that of some of the lower classes. It is declared in the Manusamhita that "Brahmans who tend herds of cattle, who trade, who practise mechanical arts, who profess dancing, singing, who are hired servants or usurers, let the judge exhort and examine as if they were Sudras."§

Another principal feature of the period under review was the gradual elevation of the S'údra class. This was effected in a variety of ways. Outside the limits of Aryan territories there reigned powerful aboriginal

*Manu, III. 142, † Manu. VIII. 37, 38.‡ Manu. III, 151 B.C.
§ Manu. VIII. 102.

princes. As the population of the Aryas increased they had to migrate and settle in the dominions of many of them, who, for reasons indicated before, were either classed with the S'údras, or described as fallen from some one or other of the three higher castes. But, however they were described by Brahmanical writers, and whatever may have been the influence of Aryan civilisation on them, politically and socially, they were far superior to the original S'údras. A dynasty of S'údra kings became paramount in Aryan India about the fourth century before the Christian era. Then again, there were a great many savage and semi-savage tribes. The Aryan authors manufactured fanciful genealogies for them, made them out to be 'mixed' or 'fallen' castes as usual, and assigned them a position below that of the Sudras. Thus the lowest caste, of the last two periods came to stand very high in the social scale, for there were now scores of castes below it. The inter-marriage moreover, between Brahmans and Kshatriyas, Brahmans and Vais'yas, Brahmans and S'údras, and *vice versa*; between Kshatriyas and Vaisyas, Kshatriyas and Sudras, and so on, bridged over the gulf that had once interposed between the original pure Aryan castes and the aboriginal Sudras, not so much, if at all, by the establishment of distinct 'mixed' castes, as that of divisions and subdivisions of the various castes.* In this intermixture and confusion of Aryan and non-Aryan blood, the loss in purity to the higher classes, was a clear gain to the lower. Thus the invidious distinction between a caste of conquerors and a caste of the conquered began to die away, and the deep stain that had once rested on the S'údra as belonging to a race, separated almost by an impassable barrier from the higher classes, began to be wiped off.

I have already told you how the Brahmanas ceased to be a priestly caste. It was only a very limited section of them that stlll continued to perform the great public sacrifices in strictly Aryan principalities. But by far the greatest majority of them, were anything but priests—ministers to kings, soldiers, agriculturists, and what not. Similar was the fate of the second or Kshatriya caste ; in fact, as we shall see, this caste, as a pure caste became gradually altogether extinct. The Vais'yas, the mass of the original Aryan population, had,

* The names of such 'mixed castes as 'Ambastha, 'Mágadha,' 'Baidcha,' are evidently derived from the territories occupied by them. The identification of 'Ambastha,' with the 'Ambastæ,' of Arrian was suggested by Mr. Wilford (*As. res.*, vol. viii., 338). The names of the 'fallen' castes 'Paundraka,' 'Odra,' 'Dravida,' 'Camboja,' 'Yavana,' 'S'aka,' 'China,' explain themselves.—Manu, (x., 8-51.)

of course, from the very first, engaged in all sorts of occupations—they were agriculturists, tradesmen, merchants, servants, artisans, and so forth. The gradual filling up of the gap between the S'údras and the higher castes went a very long way to ameliorate the condition of the former ; so that even in the dominions of the Aryans themselves, they could not have been a class of servants or a "servile" caste. But outside those dominions there were Aryanised or half Aryanised S'údras kingdoms; and it is inconceivable that Sudra princes should not have employed their kinsmen in the higher grades of the public services, or should have forbidden them to follow any other occupations than those of sevants and labourers.

You will thus perceive the utter absurdity of talking of these four castes as being "priestly," "military," "mercantile," and "servile," respectively, each with a hereditary profession. If this were the case, we cannot conceive any process by which all but a very few of a priesthood were transformed into anything and everything but priests, or by which a body of servants could have been translated into princes, noblemen, artisans, &c., or by which the "military" and "mercantile" castes became extinct as pure castes.

Then with regard to the so-called 'mixed' and 'fallen'

castes described in the Manusamhitá, the highest authority on caste. There are some 55 of these mentioned, with professions assigned to half that number, and pedigrees manufactured for them all. The fact is, all the 'fallen' castes, and most of the 'mixed' castes, are mere names based on minor ethnological distinctions, &c., given to peoples with whom the Aryans came in contact subsequent to the establishment of the hypothesis that there were but four castes at the creation; and there is abundant confirmatory evidence of this conclusion. The language of some of the 'mixed' and 'fallen' castes, as, for instance, that of the Drávidians is as different from Sanskrit, the language of the Aryans, as Hebrew is from English. There is, however, no reason, why the loss of purity to an Aryan class should be accompanied by such a radical change of language.

Then, again, there are 27 'mixed' castes, to whom professions are assigned. Of these, half-a-dozen,* that is very nearly one fourth with, of course, six different genealogies, are mentioned side by side as subsisting by hunting. These are evidently savage tribes, unless indeed we conclude that by an inversion of the natural

*Namely, 'Ugra,' 'Cshattri,' 'Pukkaṣa,' 'Andhra,' 'Meda,' and 'Sairindhra,' of Manusamhiṭa.

process of social evolution, so many tribes, following such a primitive occupation did not come into existence in India until the Aryan community had attained to a tolerably high stage of civilisation.

I have shewn you the error of the supposition, that a particular profession is confined to a particular caste, in the case of the four great castes—an error which underlies the popular notion of caste and on which the hypothesis of Mill is based. With regard to the minor castes, we find that many of them have become extinct, and that the professions of many more have radically changed. A caste of men, whose means of subsistence, according to the Manusamhita, is killing of animals that live in holes, is transformed in later books, into one of encomiasts or bards: another of attendants on women is converted into one of traders; and so on.* Had the

* 'Súta,' who is described as 'horse-trainer,' 'charioteer' in the Manusamhita becomes 'carpenter' in the Amaracosha and 'bard' in the Medinicosha.

Similarly, 'Ugra,' who is said to live by killing animals in Manu, becomes a 'bard' or 'encomiast' in the Tantras; 'Magadha,' 'a travelling merchant' in Manu, is described as 'minstrel,' in later works. Another curious instance of radical change is presented by "Vaideha," who is spoken of as 'an attendant on women,' in Manu, and as a 'trader', in more recent books.

sons of the members of a caste been compelled to follow the occupations of their fathers, we cannot understand how such transformations could have taken place. Again, nowhere in the "Institutes of Manu," or in any other work of the periods we have been treating of, do we meet with such castes as those of weavers, blacksmiths, silversmiths, barbers, &c. Had the caste system been propounded by one or more legislators to secure division of labour, as supposed by Mill, these are the very castes which should have first made their appearance. Cloths made of cotton and other materials are not only frequently mentioned in such works as the "Institutes," but there are allusions to rich and expensive garments even in the ancient hymns of the Rigveda. From the constant mention of gems, and ornaments made of the precious metals we may infer, that they were in no small demand. It is thus evident that these and similar arts and manufactures were practised by the members of the Indian community without their forming distinct castes. I wish you to bear these facts in mind, as they have an important bearing on what I shall have to say in the sequel of this lecture.

IV. & V.—BUDDHISST-HINDU and HINDU PERIOD—It is customary with writers on Indian History to divide it into four Periods, *viz*:—(1) Vedic, (2) Brahmanic,

(3) Buddhist, and (4) the Period of, Brahmanical revival. The term "Vedic" is too vague for chronological purposes; I have, therefore, substituted for it 'Rigvedic." We have seen reasons to split up the Brahmanic period into two. The designation of the third and fourth periods is erroneous and misleading. The system of Gautama, the Buddha, which, it must be carefully borne in mind, was altogether different from the so-called "Buddhism" of later times, was, like other systems of Hindu philosophy, a mixture of ethics and metaphysics. Whether, in point of numbers or of influence, his followers were very much like the followers of other developments of Rationalistic Brhámanism, as the Sánkhya, the Náyya, &c. It was in the reign of As'oka, (about the middle of the third century, B. C.) that Buddhism spread beyond the limited circle of cultivated thinkers. But the Buddhism as preached by him and as adopted by his subjects was an embodiment of moral precepts. The edicts of that large-hearted monarch clearly shew that his object was not to supersede the religions of the people, but simply to teach them morality, which he considered to be the essence of all religions. The people retained their religious beliefs, whatever they were, and at the same time declared themselves followers of the Buddha. Thus grew up

those forms of faith which are included under the term "Buddhism," but some of which had nothing beyond a nominal connection with the system of the great thinker of Kapilavastu.

During the whole of the "Buddhist" period, Hinduism was being developed and spreading far and wide. It was then that the two great sacred works of the Hindus, the "Rámáyana" and the "Mahábhárata" were composed; and the literature of that period is steeped with legends borrowed from these storehouses of Hindu mythology. About the beginning of the 5th century A.D., we have the evidence of the Chinese traveller, Fa Hian, that Hinduism flourished side by side with Buddhism. When Hiouen Thsang (another Chinese) visited India two centuries later, the former seems to have been in the ascendancy; and at Kanoj, the capital of the most powerful monarch of the time, who was a zealous Buddhist, there were as many Hindu temples as Buddhist monasteries.

The Buddhist and Hinduite groups of religion originated under similar conditions, and resembled one another in many important points. They were alike different forms of aboriginal idolatry moulded and

* See Fa Hian's Travels, translated from the Chinese by the Rev. S. Beal.

refined by Aryan culture and Aryan morality. Many of the so-called "Buddhists" were, strictly speaking, "Hindu-Buddhists", that is, Hindus who professed themselves to be followers of Buddhism when that religion was favoured by a powerful prince. There was, however, one important theoretical difference between Buddhism and Hinduism. The Buddhists disregarded the superiority of the Aryas by denying the authority of the Vedas; whereas Hinduism was professedly based upon these works. The contests in later times between the Buddhists and the Hindus turned chiefly on this point. The former had ultimately to yield. Hinduism then began to reign supreme. But no such thing as the "Revival of Brahmanism" ever took place. These few remarks will, I trust, make clear to you the impropriety of using the terms "Buddhist" period and the period of "Brahmanical revival."

I have already pointed out to you some of the most important causes which tended to obliterate the distinction between the Aryan conquerors and the conquered S'údras. The Kshatriyas and the Vais'yas, each split up into numberless impure minor castes, became confounded with, and merged into, the numerous ramifications of the S'údra and the so-called 'mixed' and 'fallen' castes. It was certain sections of the Bráhmanas alone that succeeded or claimed to have succeeded in preserving the purity of their blood to any perceptible extent. They inherited the whole of the sacred literature of the Aryas, as well as the traditions of Aryan learning and Aryan civilisation. They had now the whole field to themselves. During the Brahmanic Period their influence, as we saw, had indeed been very great. But the extravagant pretensions of the Brahmanic priesthood were, as we also saw, then disputed by the other members of the Aryan community, especially the Kshatriyas. These as well as the Vaisyas had, from the very first, enjoyed many important privileges in common with the Brahmans, and had served as the lever to Brahmanical ascendancy, but now they were indistinguishable from the descendants of the original non-Aryan peoples, and to all intents and purposes, quite dead. The secularisation of the Bráhmanas, which commenced with the movement of Rationalism still went on. But a limited section of them, having now pretty nearly all their own way, by manipulating the aboriginal forms of faith, refining and polishing them off with ideas, borrowed from Aryan theology, philosophy and metaphysics, built up a huge superstructure of idolatry and fetishism known as "Hinduism."

The religion of the Aryans as represented in the

hymns of the Rigveda, the Bráhmanas, the more ancient Upanishads and all other works of the periods we have been treating hitherto has nothing whatever to do with image worship. That Hinduism, at least as believed in by 999 persons out of every 1000, has only a nominal connection with that religion, admits of no doubt; and it is also certain that the heterogeneous forms of faith included under the general designation of "Hinduism" are chiefly the result of the Aryanisation of the non-Aryan peoples—monuments of a curious kind of successful missionary work. Two of the most important results which followed the establishment of Hinduism were, first, the formation of a priesthood mainly from amongst the Brahmans—a priesthood, however, of an entirely different character from that of the Brahmanic period. Instead of assisting at great sacrifices, they performed the worship of gods, and goddesses in temples, under trees, by the riverside, and so forth. Secondly, the establishment of Hinduism elevated the position of the S'údras still further. There was no longer a religious distinction between them and the Aryans: all became a confused mass of heterogenous Hindus.

The other more important changes which have brought the caste-system to its present condition have been chiefly effected within the last 6 or 7 centuries. It was in the twelfth century that the Mahomedans succeeded in conquering and occupying a large po.tion of India; and it is from that century that the decay of Hindu civilisation began. Eve:y work in the Aryan or Hindu literature that has the stamp of genius or originality, whether on mathematics or medicine, philosophy or philology, was written before the close of the 12th century. The Hindus gradually forgot the principles of the sciences in which their ancestors had acquired such high distinction; and several of those sciences were reduced to mere arts.

Certain sections of the Brahmans now came to be the priests and teachers, guides and advisers, of the new Hindu community. They constituted the select few who had, or were supposed to have, a knowledge of the Aryan scriptures, on which the doctrines of Hinduism are professedly based, but which are a sealed book to by far the greatest majority of the Hindus. Ignorance brought with it superstition and all its concomitant evils. Earth, air, imaginary worlds above, and imaginary worlds below, were peopled with millions upon millions of gods and goddesses, demi-gods and demons; whether with selfish motives, for earning a livelihood or not, the Brahmans patronised, fostered, and developed the worship of stones, sticks, trees, rivers, and what not. These were the dark ages of India; and they have left a lasting impression on the caste-system. Ignorant imitators are not only the most perfect imitators, but they very often go beyond their prototypes. Pedigree-making was carried on with a vengeance; the multiplication of subcastes, divisions, and sub-divisions of subcastes, went on with redoubled rapidity; restrictions more stringent than ever were put upon social intercourses. Blind followers are always the most thorough-going and the most zealous. Outside the narrow and sacred precincts of an interested group of Bráhmanas, there was no one to question or dispute their authority. Reformers rose now and then; but they were few and far between. There was no systematic attempt at reformation, such as we saw was made by the intellectual Aryans immediately after the establishment of Bráhmanism. Whatever the Bráhmanas now uttered or wrote was accepted as an infallible truth. If any Brahman wanted to countenance a particular custom of a particular tribe, he had only to declare that that custom is sanctioned by the Scriptures. But whether he was right or wrong, whether he had misinterpreted or not, very few were in a position to judge. Thus grew up several most horrible practices—

such as that of "Sutteeism", or the self-imolation of widows—practices to which our Aryan ancestors were perfect strangers, and which no Aryan writer would ever have dreamt of sanctioning. Thus sprang up an infinity of caste-rules and regulations, chiefly local, some universal, but mainly such as we would expect them to be being the productions of an age of darkness and superstition. They are something more than merely conventional or customary. Men are, more or less, slaves to custom everywhere. But, if any one, in this country for instance, has the moral courage to break through a custom which he considers to be bad and unreasonable, he will become unpopular in some circles, and probably considered eccentric in some others. But, that is all he has to dread. Thunders of excommunication, however, would be hurled against a Hindu who eats food prepared by a man of lower birth, or partakes of any forbidden article of food however necessary it may be for him, or makes a sea voyage, or contracts a prohibited marriage; and excommunication means not only that all social intercourse is cut off from him, but also that he is unable to perform any religious rites and ceremonies.

These facts will no doubt, somewhat surprise those who are strongly impressed with the immutability of

Indian institutions, and who believe, that four great castes, the "priestly," "military," "mercantile," and "servile," with, it may be, their divisions and subdivisions, have existed in India from the remotest antiquity. Hitherto the accepted creed with historians of the highest authority and the prevailing popular notion have been that, caste is a division into classes with occupations descending from father to son with the regularity of clock-work. Some historians like James Mill, in order to account for such a singular, because fictitious, institution, have had recourse to the strange theory that it was established by a self-constituted semi-divine legislator. Until quite recently such a caste-system was universally supposed to have existed in ancient Egypt. Thirty-two years ago Ampére showed the groundlessness of this supposition, by proving that the professions of priest, soldier, judge, &c., were not necessarily hereditary; and that "intermarriage might certainly take place between the sacred and military orders." We have seen a similar state of things in India. It is true, that during the Brahmanic period—a period of transition between the somewhat primitive condition of Aryan society during the Rigvedic period, and the high state of civilisation which that society reached in the Rationalistic period—it is true, that period of darkness the clergy and the nobility did form, to a great extent, two exclusive orders. But, I showed you, how, not long afterwards, the Brahmanas ceased to be a priestly caste, and how the Kshatriyas as a pure caste verged on extinction. It is true that intermarriage is placed under severe restrictions at the preseut day. But we saw how intermarriage was freely carried on in the past stages of the caste-system.

In primitive societies where division of labour has not been carried to any considerable extent, professions have a natural tendency to become hereditary. The son enjoys exceptional opportunities of qualifying himself for the occupation of his father, and the father could not leave his son a more valuable legacy than the prestige of his name. It is not unusual to find in outlying villages and towns of India, certain trades and professions pursued by particular families for many generations together. But, this is more or less the case everywhere, where demand is limited, and where, therefore, the competition for supply is also limited. In larger towns and cities, however, in India, it is by no means exceptional to find the members of one and the same caste engaged in the most divergent occupations. Nothing is more common, for instance, than to find the Brahmans, who are supposed to constitute an imaginary "priestly" caste, serving as cooks, porters, &c., to Sudras, the so-called "servile" caste. By far the greatest majority of the "priests" are unquestionably soldiers, cultivators, and various kind of servants ; and it is only a small fraction of them that perform the priestly function. Even this function is far from being their monopoly ; as it is also discharged by members of many inferior castes. Only a few of the royal families lay claim to descent from the Kshatriya caste—and their pretentions are not recognised by the Hindu authorities : the remainder belong either to Sudra or Brahmanical castes. The founders of the well-known dynasties of Scindia, Holkar, Guickwar, &c., were adventurers, sprung from the S'údra caste.

We have a very interesting account of the caste-system as it existed 300 years ago in the *Ain-i-Akbari*—an exceedingly valuable work written by a singularly able Mahomedan author, who had made the manners, customs and institutions of the Hindus his special study. He gives 10 subdivisions of the Brahman caste :—

1st—Comprises those who give charity, but do not receive it ; learn but do not teach, &c.

* *Ain-i-Akbari*, Gladwin's translation, Vol. III. p.p. 85.ff.

2nd—Those who receive charity and teach, &c.

3rd—Perform priestly function for themselves as well as for others. They learn as well as teach, bear injuries with patience, observe temperance of every kind, &c.

4th—Those who are princes, &c.

5th—Merchants, tradesmen, cultivators, &c.

6th—Those who do whatever appears advantageous to them.

7th—Mendicants who receive alms from any one.

8th—Those who are bound by no rules, and like brutes do not know good from evil.

9th—Infidels.

10th—Vile wretches (*chanda'las.*)

With regard to the Kshatriyas, the author of the *Ain-i-Akbari* says :—

"There are now upwards of 500 different tribes of Kshatriyas, 52 of whom are in esteem, and 12 are better than the rest. But at present there are scarcely any Kshatriyas to be found, excepting a few, who *do not follow the profession of arms.*" (The italics are mine.)

This is with regard to the "military" caste. As for the "mercantile" caste, he says, that there is a branch of this, the Vais'ya caste, of which there are 84 subdivisions, among whom are mendicants, men of learning, artists, magicians, handicrafts, and "such expert jugglers, that their tricks pass for miracles with the vulgar, and impose even upon those who are wiser."

I trust, then, I have made it clear to you that if caste-system were defined to be a division into classes, the members of which are bound to follow hereditary occupations, such a system has existed neither in India, nor in Egypt.

What, then is caste ? We saw that during the Rig-vedic period, two great, exclusive, ethnological, political and social castes were established—the fair Aryan conquerors, on the one hand, and the darker conquered Scythian races, on the other, with a wide gulf separating the two. I shall call this caste-system, the *primary* caste-system. Our history has been mainly a history of the vicissitudes of those two great classes, of the circumstances under which the Aryan element became all but lost in the non-Aryan—in fact, a history of the dissolution of the primary caste-system. But side by side with this disintegration, we have seen how a different kind of caste has gradually grown up, which may be described to be a system of social ranks, the result partly of a hypothesis that there were only four great classes of people at the creation ; partly of minor ethnological differences, partly of differences of occupation, wealth, and influence, and partly also of ignorance and superstition. This caste-system I shall for the sake of distinction call the *secondary* caste-system—the caste-system of modern India.

If you imagine the Norman conquerors of England to have been as distinct from the Anglo-Saxons, as they were akin to the latter, whether in point of race, religion, or civilisation, you would have an idea of what the typical primary caste-system would be. As it was, the Normans and the English did form two more or less sharply defined castes for sometime after the Norman conquest. In fact, in the history of the world, I believe without exception, whenever a community has, either through conquest or otherwise, gained power or ruled over another community, the establishment of two great castes has been the inevitable result, the exclusiveness of the castes being in proportion to their remoteness, ethnologically, religiously, intellectually and physically.

I said before that the policy of the Aryan conquerors of India which made them incorporate the subject races with their society, though on the unjust condition that these races should be excluded from many important privileges, and should occupy the lowest position in their social scale, was a humane and merciful one. And it was no doubt so, when we remember how other nations no less civilised than the Indo-A'ryas, treated subjugated peoples under similar circumstances; when we remember what measures of atrocious violence were adopted by the Spartans to "reduce the strength, and break the spirit" of the poor Helot; when we remember how several other advanced peoples of antiquity held the conquered races in slavery; when we remember, and there are men living still who could call to their memory, how the kinsmen of nations occupying the foremost place in modern civilisation, held their fellow-men in disgraceful bondage. No wonder, that the ancient Greeks who visited, travelled and studied India, exclaimed with wonder: "All the Indians are free, they having no slaves among them.........the Indians are neither slaves themselves, nor suffer any others to be slaves in their country."

Even now, in the last but one decade of the nineteenth century, after so many centuries of progress, we hear of two castes, the "whites" and "blacks," in several parts of the world. I am citing these instances not to mitigate any censure that may be justly bestowed on the Aryans for excluding the S'údras from many important political and other privileges. No. The conduct of any nation that tries purposely, persistently and systematically, to put down and trample upon another nation richly deserves to be severely censured. But my object is partly to shew that the conduct of the Aryan conquerors of India was by no means exceptional, and was even comparatively merciful, but chiefly to trace such a widespread institution as that which I have designated the primary caste-system to a common principle. That principle is, I believe, what is expressed in popular language as "might is right"—a principle which, unfortunately, has prompted the policy of many a people, and civilised people too. The ferocious tiger of the forest preys upon its weaker neighbours; and, alas! for the progress of humanity very few nations have felt much more compunction in oppressing less favoured nations. It is the work of progress and civilisation to mould, refine, suppress, and supersede nature, when and where necessary; and we hope that the base immoral principle which is at the root of the primary caste-system will one day be discarded altogether from national ethics.

CHAPTER II

HINDU CIVILISATION DURING THE MOSLEM RULE

(The "Calcutta Review," January and July 1893)

THE decay of Hindu Civilisation dates from the establishment of the Mahomedan Empire. Every Hindu work that bears the stamp of originality was written by the close of the twelfth century. Thenceforth mathematics and medicine, in which the Hindus had probably made more progress than any other nation of antiquity, were gradually reduced to empiric arts, by which impecunious astrologers and needy quacks earned a bare living. The last great name in the annals of Hindu Science was that of Bhascaracharya, who wrote his great work the *Siddhanta Siromani*, about the middle of the twelfth century. The last great name in the annals of Sanscrit poetry was that of Sriharsa, the author of Naishada, who wrote before the commencement of the thirteenth century. The last great name in the history of Sanscrit prose was that of Somadeva of Kashmir, who had written his Brihat Katha by the middle of the twelfth century. The history of Sanscrit literature, from the thirteenth century, is a blank. The few courts of Hindu kings, such as that of Bijaynagar in southern India, which escaped the grasp of the Mahomedans, still fostered Sanscrit learning; it was also kept up at such places as Benares and Nadiya. But during the five centuries and a half of Moslem Supremacy Sanscrit literature can boast of only a few commentators, such as Sayanacharya, of Bijaynagar, and Raghunundan of Nadiya.

The fact of the decline of Hindu civilisation being synchronous with the Mahomedan conquest, has led to the assumption of an intimate connection of the one with the other. That Mahomedan conquest is, to a certain extent, responsible for Hindu degeneracy, admits of no question. Alberuni, who wrote half a century before the invasion of Shahabudin Ghori, referring to Sabaktagin and his son Mahmud, who made frequent incursions into Hindustan, between (A. D. 976 and A. D. 1206)* says:—

* Alberuni's India, translated by E. C. Sachau. Vol. I. p. 22.

"God be merciful to both father and son! Mahmud utterly ruined the prosperity of the country, and performed those wonderful exploits by which the Hindus became like atoms of dust scattered in all directions, and like a tale of old in the mouth of the people. Their scattered remains cherish, of course, the most inveterate hatred towards all Muslims. This is the reason, too, why Hindu science has retired far away from those parts of the country conquered by us, and has fled to places which our hand cannot yet reach, to Kashmir, Benares, and other places."

But the Mahomedan conquest was by no means the sole cause of the decline of Hindu Civilisation. It carried the germs of its decay within it. The structure of Hindu Society had already attained rigidity before the Mahomedans established their empire. The caste system had been fully developed even long before the time of Alberuni (middle of the twelfth century). The mass of the people looked upon changes of Government with stolid indifference seven centuries ago, as they do now. They were but little affected by foreign invasions; the conquerors usually left them unmolested. Notwithstanding occasional acts of persecution by zealous bigots, toleration was the policy of the Mahomedans, from the invasion of the Arabs in the eighth century to the downfall of the Mughal Empire in the eighteenth. Casim, the first Mahomedan invader of India, referred to Arabia a question relating to toleration, the decision of which gives us an idea of the Mahomedan policy: " In the towns that were stormed the temples had been raised to the ground, religious worship had been forbidden, and the lands and the stipends of the Brahmins had been appropriated to the use of the state. To reverse these acts, when once performed, seemed a more direct concession to idolatry than merely abstaining from interferenee, and Casim avowed himself uncertain what to do. The answer was that, as the people of the towns in question had paid tribute, they were entitled to all the privileges of subjects; that they should be allowed to rebuild their temples and perform their rites; that the land and money of the Brahmans should be restored, and that three per cent. on the revenue, which had been allowed to them by the Hindu Government, should be continued by the Musalman..."*

The artisans, traders, cultivators, and labourers pursued their avocations comparatively undisturbed amidst political revolutions and changes of dynasty.

* Elphinstone's " History of India," 1874, p. 310.

They were not affected by the bustle of the political or the learned world, and took but little interest in either. While the higher castes could on an emergency, take to the occupation of the lower, the latter could never aspire to the avocations of the former: while a member of the military or of the priestly caste could pursue agriculture or trade, if necessary, a Sudra or Vaisya could never become a soldier, or a priest, or an author.

Fighting was the occupation of the Rajputs at the time of which we are treating. They fought, and often fought bravely, against the Mahomedan invaders ; no disgrace rankled more in their breasts than the disgrace of a defeat in battle. Rather than surrender, they often perished sword in hand. They were patriotic ; foreign domination was irksome to them ; but they were patriotic more from their sense of honour as soldiers than from love of their country. There was scarcely any bond of sympathy between them and the teeming millions which composed the lower castes. The mass of the people considered the maintenance of the Government the business of the Rajputs with which they had no concern. As soon as the king and his army were defeated, there was an end of all oposition. India was well-populated at the time of the Mahomedan occupation. Had not the caste system placed insuperable obstacles in the way of the elevation of the lower classes, had these classes been permeated by a sense of nationality and of patriotism, it would have been impossible for the Mahomedans to establish their empire in India. The Rajputs resisted, and resisted with all their might, but they never got the co-operation of the mass of the people, nor did they expect it. There were stout hearts among the people then, as there are now. The villagers, seven centuries ago, must occasionally have resisted the infringement of their rights, and acts of oppression by the officers of Government, as they still do. But they were as unconcerned with the personnel of the Government as they still are. They must have occasionally fought the tax-gatherers, but they were not much concerned as to whether the tax-gatherers were employed by Hindus or Mahomedans. The want of a centralised government did less harm to the Hindus than this want of a national feeling. The absence of centralisation was, in one respect, a hindrance to Mahomedan progress. The whole country had to be conquered in detail. The defeat of Prithvi Raja, of Delhi, meant only the subjugation of his territory. There were many other States, the chiefs of which offered resistance, like Prithvi Raja. Thus the advance of the invader was contested at every step. But, owing to the want of a bond of sympathy between the military and the non-military classes, as soon as the former gave in, there was an end of all opposition.

The Mahomedan conquest, as we have already observed, was, no doubt, partly responsible for the decadence of Hindu literature and Hindu science. But the caste-system was equally, if not in a greater degree, responsible for this decadence. Hindu literature and Hindu science before the thirteenth century meant Sanskrit literature and Sanskrit science. In pre-Mahomedan times, literature and science were cultivated only by the Brahmans. The great poets, the great mathematicians, the doctors, the great writers of fiction, were all Brahmans, just as the great warriors were all Kshatriyas. The mass of the people had as little to do with learning as they had to do with war. They were debarred from the study of the sacred books. Alberuni says: "Hindus differ among themselves as to which of these castes is capable of attaining to liberation; for, according to some, only the Brahmana and Kshatriya are capable of it, since the others cannot learn the Veda."* From this passage

Op. cit. p. 104.

it appears that the Vaisyas, who had formerly enjoyed the right of studying the sacred books, had lost it by the middle of the twelfth century, if not earlier. Together with the Sudras, they must then have greatly out-numbered the higher classes, as they do now. Amongst the names that adorned the courts of Bhoja of Dhar, or of Vikramaditya of Ujjain, we do not find a single Sudra or Vaisya. The vernacular dialects, the dialects in which the mass of the people spoke, had not yet been developed. Sanskrit was still the language in which books were written. These books could have had but an extremely small circle of readers, and that, only amongst the Brahmans and the Kshatriyas. To the Vaisyas and the Sudras, who formed the great mass of the people, these books were as good as sealed. Their authors lived under the patronage of Hindu kings, not by the sale of their books. When the Mahomedans swept away the courts of these kings, Sanskrit learning fled, as Alberuni says, to such places as Benares and Kashmir. The downfall of the kings meant the ruin of the learned Brahmans whom they patronised; and the ruin of the learned Brahmans meant the ruin of Hindu literature and Hindu science, just as the overthrow of the Kshatriya Rajputs meant the destruction of Hindu independence.

Till the time of the Mahomedan occupation, the Brahmans reigned supreme in the intellectual world of India. At one time, during the period when the Upanishads were composed, their right to intellectual supremacy had been disputed by the military caste. But they emerged from the struggle victorious, and in the earlier Pauraink. period, the brightest period of Hindu civilisation, they were certainly the sole possessors of the field of literature and science. They had no equals, certainly no superiors, amongst any other caste. They always led; they had never been led. They came to believe, as Alberuni says,* "that there is no country but theirs, no nation like theirs, no religion like theirs, no science like theirs. They are haughty, foolishly vain, self-conceited, and stolid. They are by nature niggardly in communicating that which they know, and take the greatest possible care to withhold it from men of another caste among their own people, still much more, of course, from any foreigner. According to their belief, there is no other country on earth but theirs, and no created beings, besides them, have any knowledge or science whatever. Their haughtiness is such that, if you tell them of any science or scholar in Khora-

* Op. Cit. Vol. I. p. 22.

san and Persia, they will think you to be both an ignoramus and a liar. If they travelled and mixed with other nations, they would soon change their mind, for their ancestors were not as narrow-minded as the present generation is." Alberuni, an accomplished and sympathetic Mahomedan, found it very hard to work his way into the subject of Hindu science, though, as he says, he had a great liking for it, in which respect he was quite alone in his time; and though he spared neither trouble nor money in collecting Sanskrit books from places where he supposed they were likely to be found, and in procuring for himself, even from remote places, Hindu scholars who understood them and were able to teach him.*

At the Mahomedan conquest the Brahmans, for the first time, came into intimate and lasting contact with a people who claimed to be their superiors; who even looked down upon them with contempt. They had communications with the Greeks and had even borrowed from them. But their relation to the Greeks had been the relation of equals to equals. But now, for the first time the haughty Brahmans had to regard as masters, men whom they had hitherto looked upon as impure,

* Op. cit. Vol. I. p. 24.

foul-fedieng, barbarians (*Mlechhas*). They were no longer courted, no longer venerated by high officials; their counsels were no longer sought after by kings. Hitherto, throughout the entire length and breadth of India, in the north as well as in the south, they had possessed the greatest influence. The favours bestowed by kings must have hitherto acted as a great stimulus for the acquisition of knowledge. But now strangers filled the thrones from which kings had smiled upon them—strangers who generally regarded them somewhat as Europeans generally regard them now. Even a sympathetic Mahomedan like Alberuni disdained to be put on a level with them. He says: "At first I stood to their astronomers in the relation of a pupil to his master, being a stranger among them and not acquainted with their peculiar national and traditional science. On having made some progress......I showed them what they were worth, and thought myself a great deal superior to them, disdaining to be put on a level with them."* Such of the Brahmans as could afford to do so, fled to Kashmir, Benares and other places. "And there," says Alberuni, "the antagonism between them and all foreigners receives more and more nourishment, both

* Op. Cit. Vol, I. p. 23.

from political and religious resources".* At such places as Benares and Nadiya, Sanskrit learning were kept up by a few Brahmans. But the great majority of them gradually became more and more immersed in ignorance. The line of demarcation between them and the lower classes gradually became less and less sharp. To the Mahomedans, Brahmans, Vaisyas or Sudras were all Kafirs. The Brahmans still received the customary homage from the lower classes. But they had no longer the strength of intellect which is begotten of self-confidence ; they had no longer the originality which is the sure indication of intellectual progress. The Brahmans were the greatest sufferers by the Mahomedan invasion. The lower classes continued to pursue their occupations as they had pursued them for ages. Even the Kshatriyas found employment in the armies of Mahomedan kings. But the occupation of the Brahmans, if not quite gone, lost all its lustre and diginity. No kingly ears now listened to their songs or their achievements in the field of science ; no kings now sought their advice. They were utterly neglected, nay humiliated. They must have considered themselves disgraced. No wonder that they retired into obscurity in

* Op. Cit. p. 22.

moody silence, or devoted their energies to the composition of frivolous stories about gods and goddesses. The lower classes were now almost their only customers. The Sudras and the Vaisyas now fed and clothed them. They, therefore, not unnaturally, did what pleased their customers best. During the five and a half centuries of Mahomedan regime the best of them could produce only a few commentaries or compilations. They had all along pandered more or less to the superstitions of the mass of people, who were mostly non-Aryans. Hinduism was the result of a compromise between the non-idolatrous worship of the Aryans, as represented in the Rig-veda, and the idolatry and fetishism of the non-Aryans; and this compromise was, at least partly, the work of the Brahmans. Just as Hinduism is a curious mixture of pantheism and fetishism, of monotheism and idolatry, of elevated sentiments and degrading superstious, so not a few of the works of the Hindus, even of the brightest period of their civilisation, are strange compounds of the sublime and the ridiculous. Varaha Mihira was a great astronomer of the sixth century. His Brihat Sanhita is certainly a great work. But anyone reading it would say, as Alberuni said,* " I can

* Op. Cit. Vol. I. p. 25.

only compare their mathematics and astronomical literature, as far as I know it, to a mixture of pearl shells and sour dates, or of pearls and dung, or of costly crystals and common pebbles."

With the Mahomedan conquest the Brahmans lost the patronage of enlightened Hindu kings, and became more dependent than ever for their living on the gifts of the lower castes with whom the superstitious part of Hinduism was most popular. The Brahmans had now to please the mob more than ever. The most enlightened amongst them were, no doubt, monothiests, pantheists, or atheists, as they still are. But they never expected, probably they never wanted, the mob to be what they were. Three centuries previously to the Mahomedan occupation, Sankaracharya had expressly preached one creed (pantheism) for the philosophic few, and another (saivism) for the ignorant many. Now the number and influence of the philosophic few were greatly reduced, while of the ignorant and credulous many remained, and increased and throve. The influence which produced the sublime in Hindu works vanished; the influence which produced the superstitious and the ridiculous in them, gradually increased. So the Brahmans, under the latter influence, produced such works as the Tantras, which give elaborate accounts of absurd and obscure practices. The science of astronomy ceased to have any higher interest than that which it had for astrologers for the purpose of ascertaining which dates are propitious for certain purposes and which dates are not; on which dates and on what hours the festivals of the people are to be held; on which dates certain kinds of food are to be eaten, and on which dates they are not to be eaten. All that was grand and noble in the Indo-Aryan literature and science gradually disappeared; and all that was base and degrading, or at best indifferent, remained and flourished.

The Mahomedan conquest was by no means an unmixed evil. It did some good. Hindu civilisation hitherto had been the civilisation chiefly of the two upper classes, the Brahmans and the Kshatriyas. To the lasting honour of the Brahmans be it said, they spread their civilising influence throughout India. It was they that lifted up the aborigines, taught them to lead a settled life, made them more humane, in one word, more civilised than they had been before. This the Brahmans did, not by brute force, but by sheer force of character and intellect. To conquer a country with the idea of civilising it, never entered their heads.

They penetrated to the remotest south, to the north, and to the east, not as conquerors, but as peaceful settlers. Wherever they went, they carried the light of civilisation. Whether it be the Dravidians of the south, or the Koch and other tribes of the east, or the mountainous tribes of the north, their traditions, their religions, their dialects, their manners and customs, all bespeak Brahmanical influence. Yet the religion of the Brahmans was not a proselyting religion. The aborigines were admitted within the pale of Hinduism, but on the condition that they would form the lowest class in Hindu Society. They were glad, nay eager, to occupy this position. The process of Hinduisation of the aborigines is still going on in such outlying parts as the jungles of the Central Provinces, and may still be witnessed. The wild Gonds, who live in the heart of the jungles, lead an unsettled and primitive life. They talk in their own dialect; they eat whatever they can get hold of; they know not the use of the plough; their clothing is of the scantiest description. But, as soon as they come within the sphere of the influence of the Hindus, they lead a settled life; begin to entertain scruples about food; forget their dialect, and disown relationship with their more primitive brethren of the jungles. In short, they are Hinduised. They are proud to call themselves Hindus, although they occupy the lowest position among them, although the Brahman would not drink water out of their hands, would even consider himself polluted by their touch.

The low caste people were considered beings inferior to the Brahmans. They could never aspire to rise to the social status of the Brahmans. It was otherwise with the Mussulmans. The meanest peasant amongst them could rise to the rank of the greatest nobleman. Mahomedans preached the brotherhood of man. Mahomedanism did not place any insuperable barrier between man and man. The lowest Musalman had a right to read the Koran and to pray in the Mosque. Not so with the Hindus. "Every action," says Alberuni, "which is considered as the privilege of a Brahman such as saying prayers, the recitation of the Veda, and offering sacrifices to the fire, is forbidden to him, to such a degree, that when e. g. a Sudra, or a Vaisya, is proved to have recited the Veda, he is accused by the Brahmans before the ruler, and the latter will order his tongue to be cut off." Yet it is a curious fact, that notwithstanding the prestige which Mahomedanism enjoyed, as the imperial religion; notwithstanding the equality which all its votaries enjoyed; notwithstanding such gentle pressure as was exerted by the imposition, at times, of a poll-tax on all non-Mahomedans, and notwithstanding such violent pressure as was exerted—though fortunately at rare intervals—by enthusiastic bigots, the religion of Mahomed found comparatively few converts amongst the lower sections of Hindu society. The fact that, notwithstanding the immigration of Mahomedans from various parts of Asia for some seven centuries or more, they still do not form more than a fifth of the entire population of India, speaks volumes in favour of the stability of Hinduism. But, though Islam failed to make any converts, it exerted a great and wholesome influence on Hinduism. It was chiefly this influence that produced that succession of earnest reformers who shed such lustre on India from the commencement of the fourteenth century to the beginning of the sixteenth. Ramananda, Kabir, Nanak and Chaitanya were certainly influenced by the tenets of Mahomedanism. They all preached the Unity of the Godhead; they all protested against caste; they all denounced idolatry. Kabir, Nanak, and Chaitanya founded large sects which have survived to the present day. Ramananda chose his disciples from among the lowest castes. He had even a leather dresser amongst them. The most distinguished of his disciples was

Kabir, a weaver. "To Ali and Rama we owe our life," say the scriptures of Kabir's sect, * "and should show like tenderness to all who live. What avails it to wash your mouth, to count your beads, to bathe in holy streams, to bow in temples, if, whilst you mutter your prayers or journey on pilgrimage, deceitfulness is in your heart? The Hindu fasts every eleventh day, the Musalman on Ramzan. Who formed the remaining months and days, that you should venerate but one? If the Creator dwell in tabernacles, whose dwelling is the universe; The city of the Hindu God is to the East (Benares), the city of the Musalman God is to the West (Mecca); but explore your own heart, for there is the God both of the Musalmans and of the Hindus. Behold but one in all things. He to whom the world belongs, He is the Father of the worshipers, alike of Ali and of Rama. He is my Guide; He is my Priest." Kabir, Chaitanya and Nanak, all admitted Mahomedans into their sects. There were Moslems who regarded Kabir as one of their own. Tradition says that on his death a dispute arose amongst his followers, composed partly of Mahomedans and partly of Hindus, as to the manner in which his body was to

* Quoted in Hunter's "Indian Empire," Second Edition p. 218,

be disposed of. Chaitanya, though himself a Brahman, denounced caste as strongly as Kabir. Several of his disciples belonged to low castes. There were even Musalmans amongst his followers.

Nanak belonged to a trading caste, which ranks below the military caste. He must have been greatly influenced by the teachings of Kabir and by the contact of Islamism. The thesis of one of his first sermons is said to have been—"There are neither Hindus nor Musalmans." Like that of Kabir, his name is still venerated by many Mahomedans.

In southern India the influence of Mahomedanism on Hinduism is distinctly recognisable at an earlier date than in Northern India. "Criticism," says Dr. Barth, "is generally on the look-out for the least traces on Hinduism of Christian influence, but perhaps it does not take sufficiently into account that which Islamism has exercised............The Arabs of the Khalifat had arrived on these shores (of the Deccan) in the character of travellers or merchants, and had established commercial relations and intercourse with these parts, long before the Afghans, the Turks, or the Moghuls, their co-religionists, came as conquerors. Now it is precisely in these parts that, from the ninth to the twelfth century, those great religious movements took their rise which are connected with the names of Sankara, Ramanuja, Anandatirtha, and Basana; out of which the majority of the historical sects come, and to which Hindustan presents nothing analogous till a much later period. It has been remarked that these movements took place in the neighbourhood of old-established Christain communities. But alongside of these there began to appear, from that moment, the disciples of the Koran. To neither of these do we feel inclined to ascribe an influence of any significance on Hindu theology, which appears to us sufficiently accounted for by reference to its own resources; but it is very possible that, indirectly, and merely, as it were, by their presence, they countributed in some degree towards the budding and bursting forth of those great religious reforms which, in the absence of doctrines altogether new, introduced into Hinduism a new organisation and a new spirit, and had all this common characteristic, that they developed very quickly under the guidance of an acknowledged head, and rested on a species of authority akin to that of a prophet, or an Iman. Now, to effect such a result as this, the Arabian merchants in the first centuries of Hegira, with the Mahomedan world at their back, were perhaps better qualified than the poor and destitute churches of the Malabar and Coromandel Coasts."*

The impetus which the reformers gave, directly and indirectly, to the progress of the vernacular literatures, was very great. In the Deccan the tenth century witnessed the production of the great Paria work, the Kural of Teruvalluvar. The Ramayana was translated into Tamil early in the twelfth century; and the Tamil Sivaite hymnologics were the production of the three centuries from the thirteenth to the sixteenth. The Marathi literature was developed about the same time as the Tamil. The first writers of note were Nanadeva and Dyanoba, who wrote about the end of the thirteenth century. Like the Tamil authors, they both wrote didactic or religious poetry.

In Northern India the teachings of Kabir and Chaitanya were embodied by their followers in voluminous works, which enriched the vernacular literatures. They preached to the people in the languages of the people. Their adoption of the vernaculars as their literary languages was a protest against the exclusiveness of the orthodox Brahmans, a small number of whom still clung to the carcase of Sanskrit. Sanskrit

* Barth's "Religions of India." London 1882, p. 211.

had no longer any life in it; it was now dead. If it was ever a spoken language and on this point eminent scholars are still divided—,* it ceased to be such about the time of the Mahomedan Conquest. The books written in it were not understood by the people; they were not meant for the people. Now the people had books written in their vernaculars, books which, if they could not read themselves, they could at least understand if read to them.

It was about the time of the Mahomedan conquest that the Indian vernaculars, the Tamil, the Hindi, the Bengali, the Uriya, and the Marathi, began to be developed. This development was not the direct work of the Mahomedan occupation. Long before that time, even centuries before the Christian era, the mass of the Hindus spoke in Aryan dialects, which were called Prakrits. Varruchi, the earliest Prakrit grammarian, enumerates four classes of these in the first century B. C.—Maharastri, Saurasim, Magadhi, and Paishachi. The vernaculars of India were gradually evolved from these dialects. They must have been in process of of evolution long before the Mahomedan conquest.

For a summary of the discussion on the subject, see Hunter's "Indian Empire," Second Edition, p. 324 et. seq.

But the Mahomedan conquest hastened the development of vernacular literature, as it also hastened the decay of the Sanskrit literature. Sanskrit was destined to die a natutal death. It was artificially kept alive by a small band of intellectual Brahmans. With the ruin of the Hindu courts at the time of the Mahomedan conquest, these Brahmans dispersed, and gradually dwindled in numbers.

The vernacular literatures would have sprung up in the natural course, because they were the literatures of the mass of the people. But the Mahomedan conquest helped their development in two ways. First by lowering the status of the Brahmans and the Kshatriyas, it indirectly tended to elevate that of the lower classes, secondly, the close contact of Mahomedanism influenced the Hindu mind so that it revolted against the inequality of the caste-system, and the domination of a hereditary priesthood. That such reformers as Kabir, Chaitanya, and Nanak were at least partly the products of Mahomedan influence, there can be no doubt; and however they might differ in details, they all denounced caste and they all preached the unity of the Godhead. The preachings of the reformers stimulated the progress of the vernacular literatures in a most marked manner. The works of the Kabirpanthis (the sect founded by Kabir) formed the greater portion of the early Hindi literature, and the contributions of the followers of Chaitanya swelled the mass of early Bengali literature.

The Mahomedan period, taken as a whole, is not quite the dark period in Hindu history which it is usually represented to be. It was during that period that such great reformers as Kabir, Chaitanya and Nanak arose and gave new religious life to a large portion of the mass of the people. They all protested against caste, and preached the equality of all men. They exerted all their strength to pull down the artificial barrier which Hinduism had set up between man and man, and to a certain extent, succeeded in doing so. Their success is not to be measured by the number of followers they have left, though that number is large. They must have indirectly influenced the lives of many who still continued to follow the banner of Orthodox Hinduism.

It was during the Mahomedan period that the vernacular literatures of India sprang up; and these literatures must have more than compensated the loss which the Sanskrit literature sustained. If the Hindus lost their Kálidása and Bhababhuti, they gained such writers as Sridhar, and Tukárám in Mahárashtra and Mukundarám Chakravarti and Rámprasád Sen in Bengal.

The loss was felt only by a few cultivated Brahmans, the gain was shared in by the great mass of the people. The Rámáyana, the Mahábhárata and the Puráns were now translated into the vernacular dialects, and could be read, or at least understood, by the people.

The Kshatriyas (including the Rajputs) fell. But in their place arose the Sikhs and the Marhattas. The Gaekwar, the Holkar and the Bhonslá who formed powerful states, all sprung from low castes. At one time they appeared as if they were going to occupy the place which had been filled by the Kshatriya in pre-Mahomedan India. As in religion, the doctrines preached by Kabir, Chaitanya and Nanak were protests against Brahman exclusiveness, as in literature, the works of such writers as Tukárám, Dádu and Rámprasád Sen were protests against the predominance of Sanskrit, so in politics the Sikh and the Marhatta powers were protests against Kshatriya ascendency. Revolutions similar to what we have briefly sketched above, took place in Budhist India centuries before the Christian Era. Buddhism disregarded caste, and adopted Pali, instead of Sanskrit as its literary language. It spread most under a powerful dynasty of Sudra Kings. But just before the Mahomedan settlement, caste-ridden Hinduism had triumphed over Buddhism. It is possible that the revolution we have alluded to above would have taken place even if the Mahomedans had not set foot in India. But there can be scarcely any doubt that it was facilitated by the practice and preachings of Mahomedanism, and by the downfall of the Kshatriyas and of the Brahmans caused by the establishment of the Mahomedan empire.

The charge of intolerance against the Mahomedan rulers of India has but a slight foundation in fact. Invaders like Mahmud of Ghazni, who had no pernament interest in the country, might plunder and destroy. But the policy of those, who, after Mahomed Ghori, settled and ruled in India, was different. They compare very favourably, indeed, with the contemporary Christian monarchs of Europe.

The persecution of Jews by Christians, of one Christian sect by another, of the protestants by the Roman Catholics, of the Roman Catholics by the protestants, of one section of the Protestants by another in Christian Europe, was on the whole severer than that of the persecution of the Hindus by their Mussalman rulers in heathen India. The horrors of the inquisition were here unknown, except, perhaps, in a small territory ruled by the Roman Catholics. Khafi Khan, himself a bigot, was shocked by the intolerant conduct of the

Europeans of his day in India, (commencement of the 18th century). Speaking of those settled in Hugli, he says : "Of all their odious practices this was the worst :— In the port which they occupied in the sea-coast, they offered no injury either to the property or person of either Mahomedans or Hindus who dwelt under their rule ; but, if one of those inhabitants died leaving children of tender age, they took both the children and the property under their charge, and whether these young children were *Sayids*, or whether they were Brahmans, they made them Christians and slaves (*Mamluks*).

"In parts of the Konkan, in the Dakhin, and on the sea-coast, wherever they had forts and exercised authority, this was the custom of that insolent people... ...They allowed no religious mendicants (*Fakirs*) to come into their bounds. When one found his way unawares, if he were a Hindu, he was subjected to such tortures as made his escape with life very doubtful ; and if he were a Musalman, he was imprisoned and worried for some days, and then set at liberty."*

It is doubtful whether the cruelties perpetrated by the Portuguese at Salsette were equalled by the most

* Sir H. M. Elliotts' "History of India" Vol. VII. p. 211.

fanatical and insensate Moslem that ever ruled in any part of India. A Portuguese armament landed at Salsette when least expected, and "carrying all before them, destroyed 1200 temples with all their images"* A new expedition was fitted out soon affer, which landed as before, "and not only destroyed the temples, but set fire to the cities, villages and all the habitations, and in a few hours reduced the whole island to ashes. The affrighted inhabitants fled almost naked from their houses and sought shelter on the shore of the neighbouring continent; and this fair scene of culture and crowded population, was converted at once into a smoking desert. Father Berno followed the troops, wielding a huge club, with which he beat down all the idols and brayed them in pieces."†

The *Jesia* (a kind of capitation tax) was the most serious grievance of the Hindus during the Mahomedan *regime*, and it was abolished by Akbar. The bigoted Aurangzeb re-imposed it. The Hindus were forbidden by him to ride in palanquins without permission. They were called upon to pay heavier duties than the Mahomedans. But the opposition which these measures

* "Discoveries and Travels in Asia" by H. Murray, p. 77.

† H. Murray. Op. cit. p. 78.

evoked shook the foundations of the empire which had been built up by the enlightened and tolerant policy of his predecessors. The Hindus all round Delhi assembled in vast numbers to pray for the recall of the Jezia. But the Emperor would not heed their complaints. One day, when he went to public prayer at the great mosque on the Sabbath, a vast multitude of Hindus thronged the road from the palace to the mosque, with the object of seeking relief. All kinds of shopkeepers from the Urdubázár and mechanics and workmen left off work and pressed into the way. "The infidel inhabitants of the city and the country round" says the orthodox Khafi Khan, "made great opposition to the payment of the *Jezia*. There was not a district where the people, with the help of *Faujdars*, did not make disturbances and resistance."*

The Hindus did not sink into political nonentity even in those parts which directly owned Mahomedan sway. They were admitted into situations of trust and responsibility. They commanded armies, governed kingdoms, and acted as ministers under Mahomedan kings. Ibrahim, the fourth king of Golconda, had

* Khafi Khan. Sir H. M. Elliott's History, Vol. VII. pp. 296-310.

Jagadeo, a Hindu for his prime-minister. Mahomed Shah Sur Adil, who occupied the throne of Delhi about the middle of the sixteenth century, committed the conduct of his Government to one "Hemu, a Hindu who had once kept a retail shop, and whose appearance is said to have been meaner than his origin. Yet with all these external disadvantages, Hemu had abilities and force of mind sufficient to maintain his ascendancy amidst a proud and martial nobility, and to prevent the dissolution of Government, weighed down as it was by the follies and iniquities of its head."*

During the reigns of the Emperors Feroksir, Rafi-ud-Darját, Rafi-ud-Doula, and part of the reign of Mahomed Shah, Rattan Chand, formerly a retail shopkeeper, enjoyed uncontrolled influence all over Hindustan. He was Deputy to Abdulla Khan, Vizier of the Empire. It was through his influence and that of Raja Ajit, that the poll-tax upon the Hindus. re-established by Aurangzeb, was abolished. "He interfered," complains the Mahomedan historian, "even in judicial and religious concerns, in a way that reduced the crown officers to the condition of ciphers. It was im-

* Elphinstone's History of India. Cowell's Ed.—pp. 460-3

possible to become a Kazi of any city, without the consent of this Hindu being previously taken."*

When Alivardi Khan became prime minister of Súja Khan, he called to his councils Raja Aalem Chand and Jagat Set, the former of whom, says Golam Hassein Khan, "possessed great merit, and deserved all the confidence reposed in him." When Alivardi Khan became Governor of Bengal, he appointed as his prime minister Jánakíram, who was a man of merit, and figured among the trustiest and most zealous of the Viceroy's friends.

Mohanlála was the minister of Surája-ud-Dewla, Governor of Bengal; amongst his other officers who held positions of trust, were Durlavram and Rámnáráyan. The Ain-i-Akbari gives a complete list of the high officers during the reign of Akbar. † The following is the number of Hindus amongst them :—

I. COMMANDERS OF FIVE THOUSAND—3.

1. Raja Bihari Mall.
2. Raja Bhagwan Das (son of Raja Bihari Mall).
3. Raja Man Sing (son of Raja Bhagwan Das).

* *Siar-ul-Mutakharin* (Briggs' Translation) pp. 89, &c.
† *Ain-i-Akbari* (Blochmann's Translation) pp. 308-326.

He was for some time Governor of Bengal. Akbar promoted him to a full command of seven thousand; hitherto Five Thousand had been the limit of promotion. It is noticeable that Akbar in raising Man Sing to a command of Seven Thousand, placed a Hindu above every Mahomedan officer.

II. Commanders of Four Thousand—2.

4. Raja Todar Mall. Though often accused of headstrongness and bigotry by contemporaneous historians, Todar Mall's fame as general and financier has outlived the deeds of most of Akbar's grandees; together with Abul Fazl and Man Sing, he is best known to the people of India at the present day. One of the most important acts associated with Todar Mall's name is, the substitution of Persian for Hindi as the court language.

5. Rai Rai Sing. He was promoted by Jahangir to be a commander of Five Thousand.

III. Commander of Three Thousand.

6. Jagannath.

IV. Commander of Two Thousand.

7. Raja Bir Bal. An entirely self-made man. He was very poor when he came to Akbar's court. Akbar

conferred on him the title of Rai Kabi(or Poet Laureate) and had him constantly near himself.

8. Raja Ram Chand Baghela.

9. Rai Kalyan Mall.

10. Rai Surjan Hádá.

V. COMMANDERS OF ONE THOUSAND AND FIVE HUNDRED—2.

VI. COMMANDERS OF TWELVE HUNDRED AND FIFTY—1.

VII. COMMANDERS OF ONE THOUSAND—3.

VIII. COMMANDERS OF NINE HUNDRED—3.

IX. COMMANDERS OF EIGHT HUNDRED—2.

X. COMMANDERS OF FIVE HUNDRED—12.

XI. COMMANDERS OF FOUR HUNDRED—5.

XII. COMMANDERS OF THREE HUNDRED—6.

XIII. COMMANDERS OF TWO HUNDRED—8.

The total number of commanders in the various grades from seven thousand to two hundred was 415, so that the Hindus filled twelve per cent. of the most responsible political posts under Akbar. The commanders named above all saw active service. Several governed important provinces; one (Todar Mall) occupied the high post of Vizier or Minister of Finance; and one (Man Sing) was raised to a distinction, which up to his time had been reserved only for Princes of the Royal blood.

Mahomedan princes sometimes took Hindu wives, and several of the Emperors of Delhi were descended from Hindu mothers. The rigidity of caste must have considerably slackened to have tempted high caste Hindus of noble families to form alliances even with the Imperial Dynasty of Delhi. It would be interesting to know how the Hindu princesses lived in the Mahomedan harem. It is said of Akbar, that from his youth he was accustomed to celebrate the *Hom* (a Hindu ceremony) from his affection towards the Hindu princesses of his harem.* Two of Akbar's wives were Hindus; and Jahangir was the son of one of them. Jahangir had ten wives, of whom no less than six were of Hindu descendant. Shah Jahan was the offspring of one of these.† He had more of Hindu than of Mahomedan blood in him.

The Indian Mahomedans gradually became partially Hinduised. Their zeal for the propagation of Islam abated. The blind bigotry of the Moslem was gradually tempered by the philosophic culture of the Hindu; and Hindu influence on the religion and Government

* *Ain-i-Akbari*, p. 184.

† *Aid-i-Akbari*, pp. 308-9.

of the Moslem, gradually became more and more marked.

The brightest period of the Mahomedan Empire was unquestionably the period between the accession of Akbar and the deposition of Shah Jahan, and it was during that period that the Hindu influence was the strongest Akbar and his most cultured Mahomedan courtiers—the brothers Faizi and Abul Fazl,—were greatly under Hindu influence.

Abul Fazl was held by some of his contemporaries to be a Hindu.* He translated the "Mahábháratâ." Akbar held the Hindu belief that it was wrong to kill cows and interdicted the use of beef.† The Hindu princesses of the harem gained so great an ascendency over him, that he foreswore beef, garlic, onions and the wearing of a beard. "He had also introduced," says Badaoni, "though modified by his peculiar views, Hindu customs and heresies into the court assemblies, and introduces them still in order to please and gain the good will of the Hindus." Raja Bir Bal is said by

* *Ain-i-Akbari*, p. 27.

† The Emperor Nasiruddin forbade the killing of oxen. Ferishta speaks of him as practising idolatry like the Hindus, so that the Koran was occasionally placed as a stool and sat upon.

some historians to have influenced Akbar in abjuring Islam. Bir Bal was the special favourite of Akbar. Badaoni says, "His majesty mourned for the death of no grandee more than for that of Bir Bal." The jealousy which the pro-Hindu policy of Akbar excited amongst bigoted Muslims was intense, and find expression in such passages as the following from Badaoni.*

" As it was quite customary in those days to speak ill of the doctrines and orders of the Koran, and as Hindu wretches and Hinduising Mahomedans openly reviled our Prophet, irreligious writers left in the prefaces to their books the customary praise of the Prophet. . . . . It was impossible even to mention the name of the prophet, because these liars (Abul Faizi and Fazl) did not like it.

" The Hindus, of course, are indispensable; to them belongs half the army and half the land. Neither the Hindustanies (Mahomedans settled in Hindustan) nor the Moguls can point to such grand lords as the Hindus have among themselvs."

The Hindu Man-Sing, Todar Mall and Bir Bal, and the practically Hinduised Abul Fazl and Faizi were amongst the most, if not the most, trusted of Akbar's

* *Ain-i-Akbari*, pp. 185, 204.

councillors. They probably contributed more to build up the Mogul Empire on a sound basis of liberal and enlightened policy than all the other officers of Akbar put together.

Tho pro-Hindu policy of Akbar was continued by Jahangir and Shah Jahan. The contest between Dara and Aurangzeb was really a contest between enlightenment and bigotry, between a pro-Hindu and an anti-Hindu policy. Dara belonged to the school of Akbar. He wrote a book attempting to reconcile the Hindu and Mahomedan doctrines. He had translatious made of fifty *Upanishads* into Persian. Like Akbar, he was considered an apostate. He is said to have been constantly in the society of Brahmans Jogis and Sanyasis, and to have considered the vedas as the word of God. Instead of the Mahomedan, he adopted the Hindu name (*Prabhu*) for God, and had it engraved in Hiudi upon rings: "It became manifest," says the author of Alamgir-nama, "that if Dara Suko obtained the throne and established his power, the foundations of the faith would be in danger."* Aurangzeb was a bigot such as orthodox Mahomedans had long been looking for; they advocated his cause, as the

* Elliott's History, Vol. VII. p. 179.

Hindus did that of his elder brother. The cause of Orthodox Islam triumphed. But the triumph was only temporary, ending with the reign of Aurangzeb.

The material condition of the people under the Mogul Empire, must on the whole have been one of ease and comfort.

The following table gives the wages of some labourers during the reign of Akbar.*

	Rs.	As.	Ps.		Rs.	As.	Ps.
Carpenters	0	2	$9\frac{3}{5}$	to	0	0	$9\frac{3}{5}$
Bricklayers	0	1	$4\frac{4}{5}$	to	0	1	$2\frac{2}{5}$
Bamboo cutters	0	0	$9\frac{3}{5}$				
Thatchers	0	1	$2\frac{2}{5}$				
Water carriers	0	1	$2\frac{2}{5}$	to	0	0	$0\frac{3}{5}$

The following are the average prices of some of the commonest articles of consumption during the same reign.†

		Rs.	As,	Ps.
Wheat	per maund	0	4	$9\frac{3}{5}$
Lentils	„	0	4	$9\frac{3}{5}$
Barley	„	0	3	$2\frac{2}{5}$
Millet	„	0	2	$4\frac{4}{5}$

* *Ain-i-Akbari* p. 225.

† *Ain-i-Akbari* pp. 62-95.

				Rs.	As.	P.
Sathi rice	per maund	...	...	... 0	8	0
Tirhi rice	„	...	...	... 1	0	0
Molh Dal	„	...	...	... 0	4	$9\frac{3}{5}$
Wheat Flour	„	...	...	... 0	6	0
Course Mung Dal	„	...	...	... 0	7	$2\frac{1}{5}$
Ghee	„	...	...	... 2	10	0
Oil	„	...	...	... 2	0	0
Milk	„	...	...	... 0	10	0
Brown sugar	„	...	...	... 1	6	4
Salt	„	...	...	... 0	6	$4\frac{4}{5}$
Onions	„	...	...	... 0	2	$4\frac{4}{5}$
Turmeric	„	...	...	... 0	4	0
Silahate cloth, per yard	...	...	...	... 0	1	$7\frac{1}{5}$
Blankets, course per piece	...	...	...	... 0	4	0

The monthly dietetic requirements of a flour-eating average adult labourer would be :—

				Price in Akbar's time.		
			Seers.	Rs.	As.	P.
Flour	...	...	25	... 0	3	9
Dal ...	...	...	5	... 0	0	$7\frac{1}{2}$
Ghee	...	...	1	... 0	1	C$\frac{1}{2}$
Salt ...	...	...	1	... 0	0	$2\frac{4}{5}$
			Total	... 0	5	$7\frac{4}{5}$

Making allowance for condiments and other little things, an adult labourer could live comfortably during the reign of Akbar on six annas per month. Taking his family to consist of five (himself, his wife, and three children), he alone being the earning member, we may take one rupee and four annas to cover his monthly expenses on account for food for himself and his wife and family. An average unskilled labourer, such as a water-carrier, in Akbar's time, would earn one rupee and fourteen annas per month. Thus he would have left a margin of ten annas to spend on clothing and luxuries,—a large amount considering the purchasing power of the rupee at the time.

The condition of the artisans must have been more prosperous than in any previous period. This prosperity was due partly to increased commerce with Europe, and partly to the taste for luxuries created by the Mahomedans. The doubling of the Cape of Good Hope by Vasco de Gama at the close of the 15th century, marks an epoch in the history of India. From that time her trade with Europe rapidly increased. Various costly gold, silk and wollen stuffs were introduced during the Mahomedan period. Satin, velvet, brocaded velvet, and broad-cloth from Persia and Europe, were amongst these.

The indigenous velvets and satins, however, held their own against those imported from abroad. These manufactures gave employment to numerous artisans. Besides raw produce, such as indigo, spices and sugar, India exported to Europe manufactured cotton and silk. These manufactures must have given employment to numerous artisans. The following are the component parts of the amount of sales by the East Indian Company in England reduced to an annual average in the seventeen years ending 1808—9.*

Piece goods	£1,539,478
Organzine silk	£ 13,443
Pepper	£ 195,461
Saltpetre	£ 180,066
Spices	£ 112,596
Sugar, indigo	£ 272,442
Coffee	£ 6,624

Muslins and calicoes used to be manufactured in almost all India, especially in Bengal and the northern part of the coast of Coromandel. Dacca was the chief seat of the muslin manufacture. The Northern Circars and the neighbourhood of Muslipatam were the most distinguished for chintzes, calicoes and ginghams. The artisans engaged in the manufacture of cotton, silk and wool were mostly, as their descendants still

* H. Murray's "Discoveries and Travels," Vol. II, p. 375.

are, Hindus; and the expansion of the European trade during the Mogul rule must have greatly increased their prosperity. The historian of Firuz Shah speaks "of the happy state of the ryots, the goodness of their homes and furniture, and the general use of gold and silver ornaments by their women.....He says amongst other things, that every ryot had a good bedstead and a neat garden."

Nicolo di Conti who travelled about A.D. 1420, describes the banks of the Ganges as covered with cities and beautiful gardens. He ascended the Ganges till he came to what he calls a most famous and powerful city named Manrazia abounding in gold, silver and pearls.* Baker who came to India in the beginning of the 16th century speaks of it as a rich and noble country, abounding in gold and silver and is astonished at the swarming population, and the innumerable workmen in every trade and profession.

Sebastian Manrique who travelled about 1612 mentions the magnificent fabrics of cotton of Bengal exported to all the countries of the East. He describes Dacca, then the capital of Bengal, as being frequented by people of every nation and containing

* Murray, op. cit. p. 12.

upwards of 100,000 souls. He travelled from Lahore to Multan through a country abounding in wheat, rice, vegetables, and cotton. The villages, he tells us, are numerous, and contain excellent inns. Tatta in Sind, where he stayed for a month, is described by him as being extremely rich. The country round is of exuberant abundance, particularly in wheat, rice, and cotton, in the manufacture of which at least two thousand looms are employed. Some silk is also produced, and also a beautiful species of leather, variegated with fringes and ornaments of silk.*

Nicholas Graaf, a Dutch physician, who travelled through Bengal in 1669, describes Rajmahal as a very splendid city. He was much struck by its mosques, temples and palaces, the gardens attached to which were considered by him to be one of the wonders of India. From Rajmahal he travelled by boat to Monghyr, and was attracted by the beauty of its white walls and of the towers and minarets which rose above. Patna appeared to him still more splendid and beautiful than Monghyr. Its trade was immense, a broad street composed entirely of shops, reached from one end of it to the other.†

* Murray, op. cit. p. 99, *et seq.*

† Murray, op. cit. pp. 168, &c.

Mandeslo, a German, who travlled about 1638, found Broach to be a populous city, almost filled with weavers, who manufactured the finest cotton cloth in the province of Guzerat. On his way from Broach to Ahmedabad, he passed through Barodra another large town of weavers and dyers. He was much struck with the splendour and beauty of Ahmedabad, the chief manufactures of which are those of silk and cotton. Cambay appeared to him a larger city than Surat, and carried on an extensive trade. He found Agra, then the capital of India, to be twice as large as Ispahan ; a man in one day could not ride round the walls. The streets were handsome and spacious ; some, of more than a quarter of a league, were vaulted above for the convenience of shopkeeper, who had their goods exposed there for sale.

Tavernier, who had repeatedly visited most parts of India, says that Shah Jehan reigned not so much as a King over his subjects, but rather as a father over his family and children. He commends the strictness of his civil Government and speaks highly of the security enjoyed under it.

Pictro della Valle, who wrote about 1623, says :—

"Hence, generally, all live much after a genteel way ; and they do it securely as well, because the king does not persecute his subjects with false accusations, nor deprive them of anything when he sees them live splendidly."*

Bernier, who resided for some time in India about the middle of the 17th century, writes deprecatingly of the wealth of the people. He admits, however, "that India is like an abyss, in which all the gold and silver of the world are swallowed up and lost; such vast quantities are continually imported thither out of Europe, while none ever returns;" and "that vast quantities of the precious metals are employed not only in earrings, noserings, bracelets of hands and feat, and other ornaments, but in embroidering and embellishing the clothes alike of the Omrahs and of the meanest soldiers."†

The Mahomedan princes and nobility led more luxurious lives than Hindoos of equal rank. They lived on more dainty dishes than the Hindoos. The names of the various rich dishes now indulged in by the Hindoo aristocracy,—such as *Qualyah, Dumpukht*, &c., bespeak their Mahomedan origin. Abul Fazl classifies cooked victuals under three heads"‡

First.—Those in which meat is used.

* Elphinstone's History of India (Ed. 1874) p. 600.

† Murray, op. cit. p. 187. ‡ *Ain-i-Akbari* p. 59.

Secondly.—Those in which meat and rice, &c., are used.

Thirdly.—Meats with spices.

He gives ten recipes of each kind, and from each recipe two to four dishes are obtainable. The Hindoos excelled, as they still do, in various preparations of sweets, in which milk in some form or other is the principal ingredient. They have also got may dishes of their own prepared from meat, fish and vegetables. These are, however, much simpler that Mahomedan dishes, the introduction of which into Hindoo dietary has been of doubtful advantage to health. Fortunately, the richly spiced Mahomedan dishes are restricted to festive occasions even among the Hindoo nobility.

Fruits were in great favour with the Mahomedans. Melons were imported from Kabul, apples from Samarcand, Kabul and Europe, and grapes from Kashmir.*

Ice came into use during the reign of Akbar, in A. D. 1556. It used to be brought by land and water from the district of Panha in the northern mountains, about 100 miles from Lahore. The average price of ice at Agra in Akbar's time was about 3½ annas

* For a list of the fruits imported in Akbar's time, see *Ain-i-Akbari*, p. 65.

per seer. Abul Fazl says, that all ranks use ice in summer; the nobles use it throughout the whole year.*

Tobacco, which is now so successfully naturalised, and is universally used throughout India, was introduced in the reign of Akbar. It is interesting to note that, drunkard as he was, Jehangir published an edict against the use of tobacco, which he considered very harmful.

Jehangir says in his Memoirs:—"As the smoking of tobacco had taken a very bad effect upon the health and mind of many persons, I ordered that no one should practise the habit. My brother Shah Abbas, king of Persia, also being aware of its evil effects, had issued a command against the use of it in Iran."†

The Mahomedans generally wore made up garments. There can be no doubt that the higher class Hindus in pre-Mahomedan times also used such garments. The sculptures of Sanchi, Amaravati, and Orissa

* *Ain-i-Akbari* p. 56.

† Wakiat-i Jahangir. Elliot op. cit. Vol. VI., p. 357. Asad Beg's narrative of the first introduction of tobacco into Akbar's Court is interesting. Akbar expressed great surprise, and examined the tobacco which was made up in pipe fuls.—See H. M. Elliott's History, Vol. vi., pp. 166-7.

show sewn dresses, resembling the *chapkan* and *Jama* of the present day. Such Sanskrit names as *Kandhuka* and *Kanchilika* for made up clothes are confirmatory of this evidence. Indeed, the occurrence of the word *suchi* (needle) and *sivan* (sewing) would indicate the existence of sewn habiliments, even so early as the period of the Rigveda.*

There can be little doubt, however, that, with the establishment of the Mahomedan rule, made up clothes (*chapkans*, *pajama*, &c.) came into more general use than before. The fact that such clothes are in more habitual use amongst men and women in the North West, within the sphere of the influence of Delhi and Agra than in any other part of India, and the fact of the greater majority of tailors being Mahomedans, are in favour of this view.† In Bengal, in Maharasthra, and in the Deccan, *dhuti* and *chadar* still form the

* See Rajendra Lala Mitra's "Indo-Aryans" Vol. I, pp. 166 et seq.

† Hiouen Thsang, the Chinese traveller to India (about the middle of the 7th century) says, that in North India "where the wind was cold, people wore close fitting garments." (R. C. Dutt's History, Vol. III. p. 143). There is some doubt from this as to how far the general use of such garments in North-Western India is attributable to Mahomedan influence.

essential components of the national costume. The practice of wearing a *chapkan* when going to Courts, if not originating with, was certainly extended in Mahomedan times.

The Hindus do not appear to have ever excelled in painting. The following interesting passage, however, occurs in the *Ain-i-Akbari.** " Most excellent painters are now to be found, and master-pieces, worthy of Bihazd (a famous painter of Persia), may be placed by the side of the wonderful works of the European painters who have attained world-wide fame. The minuteness in detail, the general finish, the boldness of execution, etc., now observed in pictures, are incomparable; even inanimate objects look as if they had life. More than a hundred painters have become famous masters of the art, whilst the number of those who approach perfection, or of those who are middling, is very large. *This is especially true of the Hindus;* their pictures surpass our conceptions of thing. Few, indeed, in the whole world are found equal to them."

Of the Hindu painters who attained fame in the time of Akbar, the following are mentioned by Abul

* Op. cit. p. 107.

Fazl: Daswanth, Basawan, Kesú, Sál, Mukund, Mádhu, Jogan, Mohesh, K'hemkaran, Tárú, Haribans and Rám. A few particulars are given of Daswanth and Basawan which are interesting. Daswanth was the son of a palkee-bearer. He devoted his whole life to the art, and used, from love of his profession, to draw and paint figures even on walls. One day the eye of Akbar fell on him; and his talent was discovered. In a short time he surpassed all other painters and became the first of the age. Towards the latter part of his life he became insane and committed suicide. Basawan is said to have been "most excellent" in back-grounding, drawing of features, distribution of colours, portrait-painting, and several other branches, so that many critics preferred him to Daswanth.

The seclusion of the upper class Hindu women in Northern India in the recesses of the zenana became stricter than ever in Mahomedan times. Long before the establishment of the Mahomedan rule, ladies had their inner apartments. They used then to rise early, clean the house, wipe the hearth, cook the food, feed the children and their husbands, and then take their meals apart from the male members of the family, much as they do at the present day. But their absolute seclusion seems to have been then unknown.*

The standard of chastity amongst the male members of the upper class Mahomedan community was never high. They were debauched to a degree. Akbar tried some peculiar remedial measures, but with what success is not known. He appointed a Daroga and a clerk to register the names of such as visited women of the town, or wanted to take them to their house. If any body wanted to have a virgin, he was required to first apply to His Majesty and get his permission. It is said that His Majesty called some of the principal women of the town and asked them who had deprived them of their virginity. After hearing their replies, some of the principal and most renowned grandees were censured, or punished, several to long terms of imprisonment.

Though the Koran abjures drinking, the royalty and aristocracy amongst the Mahomedans, especially during the Mogul period, were greatly addicted to it. All the Emperors and Princes of that dynasty, with the sole exception probably of Aurangzeb, drank, and some of them

* See R. C. Dutt's "History of Ancient India." Vol. III. P. 333.

to the greatest excess. Akbar laid down strict punishments for drunkenness and rioting. He established a wine shop near the palace, and put the wife of his porter in charge of it. He fixed the price of wine, and any sick person could get it by sending his own name and the names of his father and grand-father to the clerk of the shop. But, as Badaoni observes, "people sent in fictitious names and got supplies of wine, for who could strictly enquire into such a matter?" Babar, the founder of the Mogul dynasty, records many drinking parties in his Memoirs; and there is good reason to suspect that his indulgence in wine shortened his life. The emperor Jahangir says in his "Memoirs," that after having taken to wine-drinking, he took more and more from day to day, until wine of the grape had no effect upon him. He then had recourse to spirit drinking; and in the course of nine years he got up to twenty cups of double distilled spirits, weighing no less than six seers! * His brother Prince Danyal died of excessive drinking.

"In the brief reign of Jehandar, says Khafi Khan,† "violence and debauchery had full sway....There

* *Waki-at-i-Jahangir*, Elliot's History, Vol. VI., p. 342.

† Elliot op. cit. Vol. VII., p. 432.

seemed to be a likelihood that *kazis* would turn toss-pots, and *muftis* become tipplers." Jehandar had sunk so low, that he used to go out with his favourite mistress and boon companions in a cart to enjoy himself in the markets and drinking shops.

The vices of the courts must have had a demoralising effect upon those Hindus who were within the sphere of its influence, though the exact extent of this effect in not ascertainable.

Such social practices as early marriage and *sati* amongst the upper class Hindoos had come into vogue before the establishment of the Mahomedan rule. Even in the *Manusamhitá*, we have indications that girls were married, though under somewhat exceptional circumstances, even before the age of puberty. Widow burning is unknown both to Manu and Yajnavalkya. It was, however, a settled custom in the eleventh century; we are told by Alberuni that "Hindus marry at a very young age, and that if a wife loses her husband by death, she cannot marry another man; she has only to choose between two things :—either to remain a widow as long as she lives, or burn herself." With regard to early marriage, the Mahomedan practice must have tended to establish it more firmly.

Akbar forbade boys to marry before the age of 16,

and girls before 14, "because the offspring of early marriages is weakly.* But the mention of these orders is of the most casual character, and it is doubtful how far they were obeyed by either the Mahomedans or the Hindus.

Several of the Mahomedan emperors, however, discouraged *sati*, and adopted measures to present its abuse as far as possible. Akbar appointed inspectors in every city and district, who were to watch carefully over all cases of widow burning, and to prevent any woman being forcibly burnt. A case is mentioned in the *Akbarnama*† which strikingly illustrates Akbar's humanity and love of justice. On the death of Jai Mal (an officer in his service) his wife was unwilling to burn ; but her son Udai Sing, with a party of his bigoted friends, resolved upon the sacrifice. The matter came to the Emperor's notice and his humanity made him fear that, if he sent messengers to stop the proceedings, some delay might occur, so he mounted his horse, rode with all speed to the place, and saved the widow.

With regard to amusements, the game of *Changan* (hocky) appears to have been very fashionable with the Moguls. Abdul Fazl expresses unbounded ad-

* *Ain-i-Akbari*, p. 195.

† Elliott's History, Vol. VI. p. 69.

miration for it. "Superficial observers" says he, "look upon this game as a mere amusement, and consider it a mere play ; but men of more exalted views see in it a means of learning promptitude and decision...... Externally the game adds to the splendour of the Court, but viewed from a higher point, it reveals concealed talents." Pigeon-flying was in great favour. Presents of pigeons used to be sent by the kings of Iran and Turan. Akbar is said to have made pigeon-flying a study.

The games of *chawpar* and of *chandal mandal* were played with dice. The latter is said to have been invented by Akbar. There were, besides, the old game of chess, and various games of cards. Animal fights were encouraged by the Imperial Court at Delhi, and used to attract large concourses of people. Akbar kept one hundred and one fighting deer. The manner of fighting of this animal is described in the Ain-i-Akbari as being very interesting, its method of stooping down and rising up again being a source of great amusement. There were also buffalo-fights, goat-fights, cow-fights, and cock-fights. Betting was allowed but regulated by Akbar according to the rank of the party betting. A commander of one thousand is allowed to bet six *mohurs* on a deer. A commander of ten, however, may bet only 8 rupees on a deer.

Though against the Mahomedan law, music both vocal and instrumental, was encouraged by the Mahomedans. The Kashmir school of music was founded by Irani and Turani musicians patronised by Zain-ul-Abidin, King of Kashmir. We read of many Hindu musicians of note during the reign of Akbar, Jehangir, and Shah Jehan. Miyán Tansen was a Hindu convert to Mahomedanism; Rám Dás was for some time with Bairain Khan, from whom he once received a reward of a lâkh of rupees. His son, Sáir Das, was also a singer of note; Jagannath was one of the Court vocalists during the reign of Shah Jehan. He was weighed in silver and received 4,500 rupees. The bigoted Aurangzeb, following the letter of the Mahomedan law, ordered the dismissal of the Court singers and musicians. The historian Khafi Khan mentions a curious incident after the order had been given. The Court musicians brought a bier in front of the palace and waited so loud as to attract the Emperor's attention. He came to the window and enquired whom they had on the bier. They said, "Melody is dead, and we are going to the graveyard." "Very well," said the Emperor "make the grave deep, so that neither voice nor echo may issue from it."

SECTION III

MISCELLANEOUS

CHAPTER I

THE INDUSTRIAL CONFERENCE

(The Statesman, September 1906.)

THE institution of the Industrial Conference in connection with the National Congress marks an important stage in the economic evolution of modern India. The potentialities of the conference are great. But to convert those potentialities into actualities it is, I think, necessary that the Conference should adopt a course of action far more vigorous, practical, and systematic than what was decided upon at Benares last year. The papers read at the last Conference were all informing and suggestive, and many valuable hints can be gathered from them. But the result of the deliberations of the conference, as evidenced by the Resolutions passed by it, is extremely disappointing. Such shortcomings, however, might be expected, considering that the last Conference was the first of the kind for the whole of India; and I make these comments in the hope that they may lead to the work of the next Conference being arranged and conducted on lines more practical than that of its predecessor.

The subjects dealt with by the National Congress are generally of a nature which precludes the possibility of strong action. Year in and year out, therefore, it has had to content itself for the last twenty years with advocating reforms and recommending measures the execution of which depends upon a will which is not its own. The Industrial Conference, however, presents a wide field for action. It need not and, I venture to suggest, should not urge a single measure which it is not proposed to carry out gradually, either independently or with the help of the Government. All of the resolutions (with the exception of the last) passed at the Benares Conference are too general, too irresponsible, too vague to serve any very useful purpose at the present day; and it may be noted parenthetically that several of them are characterised by naïve simplicity not unmingled with a touch of humour. I doubt if they have appreciably edified or influenced the Government of India, or the Provincial Governments and Administrations, or the all and sundry appealed to and exhorted by them. Our countrymen should by now have got past the stage of mere recommendatory resolutions and arrived at that of steady energetic action. The educated Indians are now practically agreed that technical education should be widely disseminated, and that they should betake to industrial pursuits much more largely than hitherto. But they are mostly groping in the dark. What they want is to be shewn the way; and the Industrial Conference will, I conceive, best fulfil its function if it attempts to do that. It should in future discuss and formulate plans as to (*a*) how and where technical institutes may be advantageously established, and what special subjects may be profitably taught there; (*b*) what industries may prove remunerative, where they may be started, and how capital may be raised for them; and (*c*) how protection may be best secured for any industry which may be considered to stand in need of it. Moreover, the conference should not rest satisfied with merely propounding schemes, but should endeavour to give effect to them by means of well organised committees.

All the important industrial interests of India (including the Native States) should be focussed in the

Conference. It would, I think be well to invite delegates from the Native States,. the Chambers of Commerce, the Landholders' and Talukdars' Associations, the Mining Associations, the Tea Associations, the Industrial Associations, and the Societies for the promotion of technical education. The Agricultural, Geological, Mining, Forest, and other departments of the Government which are directly or indirectly concerned in the development of the economic resources of the country should also be approached for help and co-operation which in the present sympathetic attitude of the Government towards indigenous enterprise will, I have no doubt, be readily granted. The Industrial Conference will thus have an organisation competent enough to form well-matured plans for the economic welfare of the entire country, powerful enough to carry them out when formed, and representative enough to voice the industrial aspirations of New India. No doubt much larger funds than the allotment made at the last Conference will be required. But the Conference, under present conditions, is not likely to meet with any very serious difficulty in raising them.

CHAPTER II

Lessons in a Street

(A lecture delivered in Calcutta, August, 1884)

As we walk in the streets of this City, horses, carriages, and costumes attract our attention, nay, to not a few offer food for thought and study. But have our streets nothing else to show us ? No food for the student of Nature ? Must we go far away among hills and jungles to enjoy the company of Nature, or to study her ? Alas ! there is poor chance then forhet majority of my fellow-citizens. But they must not despair. To the blind, the most majestic mountains, the grandest rivers, and the mightiest oceans are but *tabula rasa*. But to those that have eyes, Nature reveals herself even in the traffic-crowded streets of a busy city.

Let us take a walk in a 'metalled' or 'macadamized'

street, *pákā*, as we call it. If there has been no rain for some time, we see the wind driving away dust from off the street. In dry weather this action goes on week after week almost uninterruptedly, as we must all know to our cost. If our Municipality did not water the streets several times in the course of the day, we should be half-choked by wind-blown dust. Where does it come from? Let us watch the wind, as it sweeps the street, a little more closely. We see grains of dust being blown over, and pressed against the surfaces of the hard fragments of stone or *jhámá* (over-burnt brick) which constitutes the road 'metal,' and of the larger bits of *surki* (brick-dust). If you place your hand on one of these pieces of stone or *jhámá*, you would feel that the pressure exerted by the wind is by no means inconsiderable. Now, if fine sand is forcibly driven against glass (as by a sand blast), it is etched. In a similar manner, the harder and larger materials of our streets are rubbed down and eroded by wind-driven sand; the smaller ones by being pressed against one another are pulverised. Thus a deal of dust is manufactured by wind; and in this action it is aided by drought and changes of temperature. If you picture to yourselves a dry arid country, you would be able to form an idea of the waste caused by the long-continued action of wind. In Northern China, for instance, many old fortifications have been laid bare to the very foundations by this agency. On some sandy plains of Northern America surfaces of the hardest rocks have been cut into furrows and wrinkles by it. The amount of dust carrled away by wind from a street in your presence even in one day, may seem trifling ; but if you measured the amount and multiplied it by the number of days, say, in a thousand years, you would have some idea of the important part played by the wind in the history of the world ; and what is one thousand years in the age of the earth, which stretches back to such a remote past , that we could never form an adequate conception of it ?

In rainy weather the chances are, we shall be caught in a shower. Let us take shelter somewhere, say in a shop, and look at the street. Before us is a fine sight. Innumerable runnels of muddy water trickle down the slopes into the gutter on either side. The middle and comparatively level portion of the street is a kind of miniature *watershed*; and the runnels flowing from it, miniature *rivers*. Each drop of rain as it falls contributes to the volume of some one or other of these runnels. One rain-drop, by itself quite insignificant, would but barely moisten an infinitesimal portion of the street. But what great work does it perform, what a mighty force does it become in combination with its fellow drops! Are not those runnels formed by the rain-drops? See how they swell! how they run faster and faster as the shower continues how they are carrying, pushing along their course the hard, heavy fragments which, as I have said before, constitute the road 'metal'! Rainwater is very pure. But we see the water of the runnels is muddy. Why so? You will, I know, at once answer, because it is mixed with the dust of the road. Yes, the rainwater is carrying away the fine, invisible particles in suspension and driving the heavy and more conspicuous 'metal' along the bed of the runnel. All these substances, fine or coarse, light or heavy, carried by the rainwater, are known as *sediment*.

But is that all? Is rainwater a mere transporting agency? Let us see. Stretch out your hand outside; you will feel that the rain falls with some force. If you observe a fine sandy soil after a drizzle or light shower, you will find its surface covered all over with small hollows. These hollows are called rain-prints. How are they caused? A little reflection will enable you to answer, that they are caused by the displacement of the sand, which has been pushed aside by the rain, and may be seen piled up round the rain-prints. The shower we are witnessing is a much heavier one, and is far more potent. The downpour before us must be loosening and setting going the lighter materials of the street, such as sand and *surki*, which form the sediment held in suspension in the water of the runnel and render its water impure. We have already seen how some of the heavy stones are carried by the runnels. What about the rest of the stones, those that we see projecting there, looking as if they defied the rain, as if they were immoveable? But, are they really so? You want to see for yourself the actual state of things. Very well; nothing more praiseworthy. Rational scepticism is the first condition of acquiring accurate knowledge; and such knowledge gained by observation and experiment is scientific knowledge. Take as little on trust as possible; always try to verify what you are taught.

As the shower is wellnigh but not quite over, let us go near the runnels and watch their action. Their current is not so strong as it was a little while ago; their water too is much clearer. You notice fine particles of sand, &c., being swept over and around the big stones, or pieces of brick, the road 'metal' as they are called; and these are being eroded, polished 'water-worn' as we say, just as we saw they were by the wind-driven sand. Now, the stones when they were first placed in the street were angular and possessed sharp edges. But at present, you notice the angles and edges have been considerably smoothed down. They owe this condition partly, it is true, to carriage wheels, horses' hoofs, and our boots; but these can affect them on their uppermost surface only. That they are worn, abraded, and polished to a great extent by wind-and rain-driven dust and sand, there can be but little doubt. As the finer material surrounding the stones are loosened, ground down, and washed away, their sides and lower surfaces are attacked by the rain until they yield. They are then removed and ultimately carried into the gutter at the side, forming the coarser portion of the sediment deposited there. Thus rainwater is not only a sediment-carrier, but is also a sediment-manufacturer. Sediment, you know now, is formed by the waste of the street. On a larger scale it is produced by the waste of the rocks forming the crust of the earth—the sediment that renders the water of our rivers muddy—the sediment that is carried to the sea, and forms new land, as at the mouth of the Brahmaputra, in the Bay of Bengal.

We see in the middle, rather flat, portion of the

road the 'metal' is not so liable to destruction as along the sloping sides, where it is exposed most prominently to the view. It is here, at the sides, that the runnels are manufacturing and carrying away most detritus ; it is here that the rain commits the greatest havoc. The middle portion is by no means safe. It too is wasted, only to a less extent than the sides. What is the cause of this difference ?

Let us single out a good-sized runnel. We have already called it a 'miniature river.' Its resemblance to a river will at once strike you. Like the Bhágirathi, with which we are all so familiar, it is never straight, but flows in curves, or 'bends' as they are called. Watch it closely. It is worth watching, for it is highly instructive. Here the cause of the curvature is quite apparent, which is not the case with the Bhágirathi. "The stronger survive the weaker" is a well-known law of nature. You see the water of the runnel is being turned away by the stronger stones. See it is working its way through the softer materials ; the weakest suffers first, and suffers most. It is thus that the curves are produced.

You notice that the curves are more numerous in the flatter middle portion. That is because there the runnel is rather weak, cannot overcome even comparatively slight obstructions, and is turned away from side to side. There the water is comparatively still. Look at those bits of sand and *surki* in the bed of the runnel. They are hardly moving and being deposited at the convex side of the 'bend,' the side where road 'metal,' on account of the resistance offered by it, projects into the runnel, where the water is stillest. This is exactly how *chars* are formed along the banks of the Bhágirathí; you will invariably find these *chars* on the convex side of the curve, where the water lingers and drops its sediment, the main current sweeping round and breaking away the opposite bank.

There again, in the bed of the runnel, you see the grains of sand have met with an obstruction; they have come to a standstill there; the current has not the power to carry them any further. More grains come; they gather together; an island is gradually formed. This is exactly how island *chars*, of which some of you may have noticed magnificant examples in the *Bhágirathí*, as at Sántipur and at Tribeni, are formed. Here, in a few minutes, you have traced the history of one of the most prominent physiographical features of the rivers of Lower Bengal. The process is the same; the difference is only one of magnitude and of time.

Along the lateral portion, nearer the gutter, you

observe the current is stronger. It forces its way through materials which would have obstructed its course on the flatter middle portion. The runnel has been joined by numerous runnelets, and its volume is greater; its course here is not so full of curves, but is comparatively straighter. The grains of sand and *surki* are moving more swiftly;—see they are running; fragments of the road 'metal' too are being carried along. Observe there is but little of the *chars* you noticed a little while ago; nothing is allowed to rest; all obstruction is overcome; everything is carried before the mighty runnel. Here it is comparable to a hill-stream flowing down a slope, not to a meandering river. There is little deposition of sediment in it, or along it; all is driven into the gutter below. The destructive action of the rain, therefore, is most marked here. But the difference is only one of degree; the whole street suffers waste more or less. The waste, as you must now clearly see, is proportional to,

(1) The volume and velocity of the current.

(2) The size, shape, and specific gravity of the materials.

We have hitherto confined our observations to the surface action of the rainwater. Now you all know it permeates the soil and subsoil, nay sinks down deep into the crust of the earth through cracks and crevices in the rocks. The water which comes out in tanks, wells or springs is this underground rainwater. We have no opportunity here, in the street we are considering, of studying its action well. But in old neglected roads, especially in those that are *kâtchâ*, *i.e.*, not 'metalled,' you may come across small *Landslips*. These are due to the destructive action of underground water, as are indeed the landslips of which we read in the papers as occasionally taking place on the Darjiling-Himalayan Railway and other mountainous regions.

Again, we have as yet been speaking of the mechanical action only of the rainwater. Now, many of you must have read in books on chemistry that rain absorbs a little air in its descent to the earth. With the air it takes in its impurities also; and among these carbonic acid plays an important part. But the chemical action of rain cannot be so well studied here; and we shall not dilate on it.

The havoc done by the shower we have just had may seem quite trifling to you. But a little reflection will show, that, in rainy weather, shower after shower, day after day, week after week, month after month, must cause an amount of waste by no means insignificant. If this street were left to itself by the Municipality for five years, and if you compared its condition at the end of that period with its present state, its waste would, then, I am sure, strike you very forcibly. The rate of waste is slow but sure. Great things are always done slowly; great works take time to accomplish. A gentleman seeing the heaps of stones that are annually placed on our streets by the Municipality, said, that these will in time overtop our houses. But the Municipality only repairs the damage done by wind and rain. The amount of stones put in our streets every year is a kind of measure of the waste they suffer; and what an enormous waste that is! If a street were left quite unrepaired for a few years, it would be lowered, become full of pools and channels, and be rendered quite unfit for traffic. The rails of our tramways were originally placed nearly on a level with the street. But how do they stand now? (July, 1884). Several inches above the street in some cases, so that complaints of damage done to carriage wheels in crossing them have of late been appearing in the newspapers. I need not tell you now the causes that have led to this state of things. The manager of the Tramways says, that the present rainy weather is very trying, that he has gangs of men working, but they cannot keep pace with the destruction caused by rain ; they cannot cope with the forces marshalled against the Tramway Company by Nature, so much material is washed away from the street every day !

The havoc caused by such agencies as wind and rain to the crust of the earth is called by geologists *Subaerial denudation*—an expression which it is necessary for you to remember, because you frequently meet with it in books on Geology and Physical Geography. The denudation which we see effected before us in one day, or in one year, or even in the lifetime of a man, may be almost imperceptible. We do not quite ignore it, however, for we pay heavy rates to our Municipalities to keep our roads in repair. But we do not carry the operations we are witnessing to their logical conclusion ; we do not consider their magnitude, do not reflect on their importance. If we estimate the amount of sediment transported by rain-water from a street in one year—and such an estimate could be made—and multiplied it by a million years, the result would be very striking ; and what is one million years in the age of the earth ! It has been calculated that the drainage-basin of the Ganges above Ghazipur is being lowered one foot in eight hundred and twenty-three years through subaerial denudation.

At this rate it would take 930,000 years to reduce that area to the sea-level. At the end of that period the Himálayan region would be flooded over by the sea by the continued operation of agencies which we see at work around us every day ! High hills, which look as if they have been where they now are from the beginning of the world, and will stand there to eternity, which raise their heads boldly and proudly high up in the sky defying rain and wind, will one day be disintegrated and levelled down ! How many Himalaya-like mountains have been reduced to mere knolls and bosses ! how many have disappeard altogether !

Hill and dale, brook and river, have all been carved out by subaerial denudation. All the grand sublime sights, which charm the traveller in mountainous countries, owe their origin to it. Let us look at the street again. It may sound rather ridiculous to speak of mountains and valleys and of a city street in the same breath. Here we have nothing that is grand or sublime, no scenery to speak of; but the street teaches us lessons, which, owing to their magnitude and complexity, high mountains and wide valleys fail to impart.

Observe those two pieces of road 'metal,' how they stand up, the fine material between them having been washed away. Each of them is a miniature hill, and the gap produced between them a miniature valley. If you fully comprehend how this hill and this valley have been formed, you would have no difficulty in understanding the origin of a great many hills and valleys in nature. These are on a much grander scale, certainly; but the causes that have produced them are essentially the same as those whose operations we have been witnessing.

The two fragments of 'metal' we have singled out were originally covered up by *surki*, so that they were then not at all visible. The wind and rain first removed the *surki* from their top, and then from their sides, and from the space between them; they now stand up as *Hills*, because they have withstood denudation better than the weaker, finer material surrounding them. The space between them, which consisted of such material, is now a *Valley*. In nature we have hard and soft rocks forming the crust of the earth. The former resists denudation better than the latter, and therefore stand out longer, just like our road 'metal,' and form hills; while the softer rocks are denuded away more quickly, exactly like the *surki* of our street, and the tracts occupied by them become valleys.

Each runnel has its *drainage basin*. Look how it is joined by those runnelets, its tributaries; each of these has its own little valley scooped out by it. All these little valleys open into the main valley—that of the runnel. Now this valley, which also, I need hardly tell you, has been gradually carved out, extends in the directions of the slope nearly down to the gutter. You thus learn that the slope of the ground is an important factor in the formation of valleys. The valleys of the Narbada and Tapti, for example, run east-west, the direction in which the rivers flow,

The portion of the street denuded and drained by each runnel and its tributaries constitutes its drainage basin. This drainage area, you will observe, extends close down to the gutter. But just before entering it, and for some distance in it, the runnel moves sluggishly through the sediment deposited by it, branching out into a number of channels. This fan-shaped area, which has been built up by the sediment deposited by the runnel, is its *Delta.* You notice a striking resemblance between it and the *Sunderbun*, which is the latest formed portion of the *Delta* of the *Ganges.*

But we have not time to-day to learn the lessons taught by the gutter, the receptacle of the detritus dropped by the runnels at their mouths. These may very well engage our attention another time.

CHAPTER III

NOTE ON SOME EARTHEN POTS FOUND IN THE ALLUVIUM AT MAHESVARA (MAHESAR)

(Journal, Asiatic Society of Bengal, Vol. LI. pt. I., 1882)

MAHESVARA is the capital of the southern portion of Holkar's territory known as the Subhá of Nimar, and is situated on the Narmadá some 40 miles south of Indore. Modern Mahesvara rose into importance during the reign of Ahalyá Bái who made it the seat of her government. As containing the ashes of that remarkable and venerable woman it is largely resorted to by pilgrims.

Captain Dangerfield in his paper on the Geology of Malwa* mentions having been shewn in the alluvium at Mahesvara large "earthen vessels and bricks," which were stated "to have been, at a very remote period, overwhelmed by a shower of earth." Since Dangerfield's time, however,—and he wrote more than 60 years ago—no one has taken any notice of them. I happened

* Malcolm's "Central India," Vol. II. p. 325.

to pass through Mahesvara last April, and wanted to avail myself of the opportunity to examine the antiquities in question. I was located in a bungalow to the west of the town. The upper 6 feet of the alluvium upon which the bungalow stands, is composed very largely of broken pottery, and I extracted a nearly whole urn-shaped earthen pot, quantities of more or less damaged cup-shaped vessels, fresh water shells, fragments of lower jaw and bones of Ruminants, &c. The pottery remains had evidently been carried by the river from some place higher up; and I learnt on inquiry, that at the eastern extremity of the town, there were to be seen by the river side the remains of an ancient city turned upside down, as my informant stated, through supernatural agency. The banks of the Narmadá at the place (known as the "Mandal kho") are some 65 feet high. Approaching it by boat, one sees from a distance two well-defined beds of unequal thickness, the upper (about 20 feet) remarkably light-coloured, and the lower (about 45 ft.) of a brownish hue. On getting to the place, my guides pointed out towards the base of the upper bed portions of pottery-work, no doubt as they had been pointed out to Dangerfield three-score years ago, and are described by him as large earthen vessels. The pottery appeared to enclose round wells, of which I counted half-a-dozen. They are all more or less inaccessible, and it is not without considerable difficulty that I managed to clamber up to one.

The two zones of the alluvium just mentioned are separated by a thin stratum of very dark-coloured clay which to all appearance formed the soil of the now inhumed city. The lower portion (6 ft.) of the light coloured upper zone contains bits of charcoal and fragments of pottery in abundance. The presence of the former would lead one to infer a large admixture of ashes. Pieces of human and cattle bones, small pebbles, bricks and a few large rolled pebbles chipped off artificially were obtained from this bed. The overlying alluvium (about 14 ft.) is characterised by the entire absence of these, and the occurrence of large rolled pebbles and freshwater shells. The pottery-work seen from below is found on examination to be composed of very thick, closely fitting circular pieces open at both ends, measuring 5½ in. vertically, and with a diameter of a foot and a half. From the well enclosed by this pottery I dug out a very large number of earthen pots of various shapes and sizes piled up with their mouths downward, some quite empty, others filled partially or entirely with an argillaceous material. The length of the vessels varies from 11 to 7 inches, and the diameter from 8 to 6; the diameter of the mouth which is without a lid ranges between 5 and 3 inches. There is no ornamentation except an unsymmetrical furrow or two an inch below the neck.

The contents of the pots when not empty are an indurated marl presenting a vesicular appearance, and containing bones of birds and small mammals and fragments of charcoal. The vesicles are irregularly elongated, and are encrusted over with a thin yellowish-brown substance which Mr. Mallet of the Geological Survey (who very kindly analysed a specimen) considers to be the remains of some decomposed vegetable matter. Large numbers of ribs probably of goats and sheep and some teeth were got mostly from the interstices between the pots. The entire absence of human bones or human teeth from inside the well is notable.

The well dug into goes down about 10ft. into the lower zone of the alluvium, though the boundary-work of pottery is carried only 2 feet downward. Earthen pots were found from top to bottom all, as remarked before, with their mouths directed downward.

As the other wells were quite inaccessible, they

could not be opened up without excavations on a large scale for which I had no time. If similarity of appearance might justify us in inferring anything we would infer them to contain earthen vessels also similar to those obtained from the well just described. It would be extremely desirable to examine them, especially as excavations may lead to important discoveries and throw some light on the early history of India. I may mention in this connection that I noticed at one end of the section, at "Mandal koh," two rows of bricks as if they enclosed the door of a house.

The points which present themselves for determination are—

(1) The age of the inhumed town.

(2) The purpose for which the well described in this paper was constructed, and the earthen vessels placed in it.

(3) The cause of inhumation.

I have not been able to settle any of these important questions to anything approaching satisfaction. I shall, however, throw together a few notes in the hope that they may be of some service to the archæologist.

The shape of the earthen vessels is quite peculiar, and the potters of the district have long since ceased to make anything like them. When we consider, besides, the thickness of the alluvium covering the wells, and of the pottery-bed below the bungalow, as well as the age of modern Mahesvara itself which is built upon these deposits and is at least some four centuries old,* we can have no doubt about the antiquity of the inhumed town. That there was an ancient city of the name of Mahesvarapura or Mahesa-Mandala, there is fair historical evidence to prove.† It is possible that the relics now discovered mark the site of that city.

Cautley in his account‡ of an ancient town discovered near Saharanpur speaks of a well near the site of that town from which "a great quantity of

* The inscriptions at Kalesvara and Matamgesvara, the two eldest temples at Mahesvara bear the dates Samvat 1622 and 1623 respectively. An inscription in a mosque near the fort deciphered to me by a Munshi gives 800 *Hijra* as the date of its erection.

† Mahesvara has been identified by Cunningham with the *Mohishifalopulo* of Hiouen Thsang. ("Ancient Geography," p. 488.) The 'Mahisa Mandala' to which a Missionary was sent by Asoka in B. C. 240 (Turnour "Mahawamso," pp. 71-73) is probably present in the names Mahesvara and Mandalesvara which are only four miles apart.

‡ Journal of the Asiatic Society of Bengal, Vol. III., for 1834, p. 225.

gharas or waterpots were taken out whole, as if," says he, " they had fallen into the well and sank." He does not, however, describe them or their contents, nor does he tell us how they occur. Their large number, and the circumstance of their having been taken out whole, make their occurrence by mere accident extremely improbable, and incline me to suspect that they were, like the earthen pots under notice, placed in the well by human hands, and for one and the same purpose. But what could this purpose be? In the present instance certainly, the wells could not have been village wells, for in that case there would not have been so many of them close together especially so near the river. Nor could they evidently have been meant for irrigation purposes. The most eligible hypothesis that has presented itself to me is, that the *gharas* were dedicated to the dead, some with the ashes after cremation, and others with cooked cereals and meat. The ashes would explain the presence of bits of charcoal in the marly contents of the *gharas*. The vesicular texture of these contents, and the peculiar lining encrustation of the vesicles could be satisfactorily accounted for by the mixing up of the cereal grains with marl brought into the pots by infiltration and their subsequent decomposition. The evolution of gases during this process would, as observed by Mr Mallet, cause the vesicles to be diverse and irregular; and such is found to be the case. Some at least of the bones found are probably the remnants of dishes of animal food.

Preserving the ashes after cremation and supplying the dead with cooked food, were practices in vogue with many tribes, both Indian and extra-Indian. Major Mockler, for instance, describes some earthen pots from Makran,* in which he says the dead were supplied with cooked food. But in this and similar cases the urns or pots occur in well recognizable and indisputable graves. In the instance at hand, however, the pots are extraordinarily numerous, and their mode of occurrence quite peculiar.

The Thero Mahadeva who was sent by Asoka in B. C. 240 to Mahisa Mandala is reported to have made 40,000 converts to Budhism, and ordained 40,000 more as priests. Hiouen Thsang, however, describes the people of the kingdom of Mahesvarapura as heretics, the most numerous being the *Pâsupatas.*† So that if the

* Proc. A. S. B. for July 1877. The vessels found by Major Mockler now in the collection of the Indian Museum are not unlike those which form the subject of this paper.

† "Hist. de la vie de Hiouen Thsang" pp. 414-415.

well had anything to do with Buddhist funeral rites, it must have been sunk either before, or during the earlier centuries of the Christian era. But as the Buddhist topes hitherto discovered are to my knowledge of a quite different structure from the well-tope at Mahesvara (if tope indeed it be), I am inclined to think that the latter was the work of some non-Buddhist Scythian tribe in which case too the date could not be later than that just surmised.* I have not, however, discovered any certain traces of such a tribe. The Bheels, the aboriginal people of the district, burn their dead, expect infants and adults who die from unnatural causes.

Dangerfield speaks of a shower of earth as the cause assigned for the inhumation ; I was told that the place had been overturned. These traditions probably point to an earthquake which might cause submergence, as in the case of the fort and village of Sindru on the Indus.†

The collections consisting of *ghards*, bones, &c., have been presented to the Indian Museum.

* James Prinsep from an examination of the coins discovered by Cautley assigns the early centuries of the Christian era as the date of the destruction of the ancient city near Saharanpur.

† Lyell's "Principles of Geology," 10th edition, Vol. II., p. 99.

CHAPTER IV

NOTE ON MAHISHMATI OR MAHESVARA (MAHESAR) ON THE NARMADA, AND THE IDENTIFICATION OF HIOUEN THSANG'S 'MAHESVARAPURA'

(From the Proceedings, Asiatic Society of Bengal for July & August, 1883)

LAST year in a short paper on some pottery found at Mahesvara on the Narmadá, I cited the authority of General Cunningham for its identification with the "Mo-hi-shi-fa-lo-pu-lo" of Hiouen Thsang. On a subsequent reference to his work, however, I found that his "Mahesvarapura" is quite a different place, the limits of its territory being fixed approximately as extending from Dumoh and Leoni (?) on the west to the sources of the Narbada on the east."†

Mahesvara (the place of my finds) being, as will be shewn in the sequel of this note, a city of great anti-

* Journ. As. Soc. Vol. LI. part I., p. 228.

† "Ancient Geography" p. 489. 'Leoni' is probably a misprint for Seoni.

quity, and the only one of that name on the Narmada, I concluded, with culpable haste no doubt, that it must be identical with the "Mahesvarapura" of General Cunningham, and omitted to examine his description closely.

The place identified by this eminent archæologist is known as Mándlá or Garh-Mandla, south of Jabbalpur, also on the Narmadá like our Mahesvara, but no less than 300 miles to the east. The ancient name of Mándlá is given as Makawati* by Tod. Sleeman in a paper on the "Gurha Mandla Rájás" in the Journal of the Asiatic Society† spells this as "Mahikmati"; and General Cunningham changes it to "Máhishmatipura," though quoting Sleeman as his sole authority.

Granting this alteration to be warrantable, it is nowhere mentioned as "Mahesvarapura" or "Mahesvara," and unless it could be shewn that this name was also applied to ancient Mandla, the identification of Hiouen Thsang's "Mahesvarapura" with it is certainly questionable.

Starting from Jajhoti (modern Khajura), a journey of 900 li to the north is stated to have brought the

* "Rajasthan," Vol. II., p. 445, (quoted in the Central Prov. Gaz. Introduction, p. l.)

† *Op. cit.* for 1837, p. 622.

Chinese pilgrim to Mahesvarapura.* General Cunningham proposes to read this as "900 li (or 150 miles) to the south," in which position he finds Mándlá. But he, having got the pilgrim there, does not find any means of getting him out of it. The following passage concludes the notice of Mahesvarapura in the Memoirs :

"En sortant de ces pays, il revint dans le royaume de Kiu-tche-lo (Gourdjdjara), puis il reprit la route du Nord. Aprés avoir fait dix neuf cents li à traverse des plaines sauvages et des déserts dangereus, il passa le grand fleuve Sintou, et arriva au royaume du même nom."

Now, Gurjara [Kiu-tche-lo] to which Hiouen Thsang returned from his Mahesvarapura is nearly 600 miles from Mandla in a straight line; whereas the language of the text just cited would convey the impression that the two kingdoms were in close proximity. Besides, it is not likely that he would go so far out of his way to visit a heretic town of comparative insignificance, as Mandla must have been at the time.

Again, the pilgrim distinctly states that the king of Mahesvarapura was a Bráhmana. On the other hand, we have the unquestionabte testimony of an inscription

* "Memoires de Hiouen Thsang," II. p. 169.

that the king of Mandla at the time of his visit was of Gond Rajput descent,* whose highest pretensions could never have risen any higher than the style of a Kshatriya; and a cultured traveller of Hiouen Thsang's stamp would surely know the difference between Kshatriyas and Bráhmanas.

M. L. Vivien de Saint Martin identifies Mahesvarapura with Mácheri.† It is 130 miles north—10° or 15°—west of Jajhoti. The distance and bearing agree as closely as may be expected with that given in the Memoirs, *viz.*, "150 miles to the north." Besides, its position harmonises remarkably with the statement in the "Memoirs" already quoted, *viz.*, that leaving the territory of Mahesvarapura, the pilgrim re-entered the kingdom of Gurjara. The eastern boundary of this kingdom, which is given as extending from Junjhnu to Mt. Abu along the Aravalis,‡ is only 100 miles from the town of Mácheri, and must have touched upon the western limit of the kingdom of that name as its circuit is given as 500 miles.§ I think, on the whole, the

* Sleeman, Journ. As. Soc. 1837, p. 625. The reigning king at the time was either Gopal Sa or Bhopal Sa.

† *Op. cit.* p. 408.

‡ Cunningham, *op. cit.* p. 312.

§ Cunningham, *op. cit.* p. 489.

probabilities are in favour of M. L. Vivien de St. Martin's identification.

General Cunningham also considered the Mahesa-Mandla to which Asoka sent the Thero Mahádeva to be the same as Mandla. There is absolutely no proof whatever that the place, if anciently called by this name, ever had Mahesa for a prefix. Besides, so early as B. C. 240, Mandla was probably a place of little importance. On the other hand, my supposition that "Mahesa-Mandala" is probably preserved in the names "Mahesvara" and "Mandalesvara," which are only four miles apart, also rests on very scant data.

The proofs of the antiquity of our Mahesvara, however, are overwhelming. I did not cite them as they are chiefly of a traditional character; but I find their cumulative evidence to be by no means inconsiderable.

Mahesvara was anciently known as Máhishmatí after Mahishmat, seventh in descent from Yadu.* The city is called by this latter name in inscriptions dated so late as the time of the Emperor Akbar. A small river which joins the Narmadá east of it is still known as Máhishamatí.

Máhishamatí was visited by Sahadeva during his

* Wilson's Vishnu Purána, Vol. IV., p. 54, (Book IV., Ch. XI.).

campaign of conquest.* It is also noticed in the Mahábhárata, *Udyogaparva*,† as well as in the *A'di-*, *Vana-*, and *Anusàsana-parvas*, chiefly in connection with the thousand armed Kártavíryárjuna. In the last named parva he is described as "lord of this whole world, living in Máhishmatí. This Haihaya of unquestioned valour ruled over the whole sea-girt earth with its ocean and continents."‡

Rávana, the king of Lanká, is mentioned in the Purána§ as having been taken prisoner at Máhishamatí by Kártavírya and kept confined like a wild beast in a corner of the city.

When Kártavírya lived it is impossible to tell. He seems to have been the contemparary of Rávana and Parasuráma, and so many anecdotes of supernatural strength have gathered round his name that he appears to us almost as a mythical personage. Nevertheless, it is surprising how numerous are the traditions still preserved of him at Mahesvara. There is a well-known fall, a little below the city, which is called Sahasradhárá

* *Mahábhárata*, *Sabháparvan*, verses 1124, 1130, &c.

† See Wilson's *Vishnu Purána*, Vol. II., pp. 166-67.

‡ See Muir's Sanskrit Texts, I. pp. 448, ff.

§ *Op. cit.* IV. II., 3. The Bhágavat Purána relates the same story. See Muir, *op. cit.* Vol. I., p. 478.

after the thousand-armed king. And what concerns us more closely, the ruins at *Mandal kho* are still held to be those of his capital—the ancient Máhishmatí or, as it is popularly known, the *Sahasra-bahu-ki-basti.*

Col. Wilford identifies Máhismati as Choli-Mahesvara,* which is identical with our Mahesvara, Choli being a small town four miles to the north of it. Fitz-Edward Hall who paid a visit to the place confirms this identification † and Col. Tod ‡ also mentions Mahesvara as "Sahasravahuka basti."

* As. Res. IX., p. 105.

† Wilson's "Vishnu Purána," Vol. II., p. 167.

‡ "Antiquities of Rájasthán" (Vol. I., p. 39, note) quoted by F. Hall, Vishnu Purána, IV., p. 59.

CHAPTER V

AN EASTERN VIEW OF WESTERN PROGRESS

From the Westminster Review, 1901, and East and West, 1902

NATURAL Science is the foundation-stone of modern civilisation. The last century boasts of more inventions than all the previous centuries of human history put together. Science has done many wonders, and promises to do many more. It is moving on and on: the goal of scientific and industrial progress of one generation becomes the starting-point of the next.

After the close of this remarkable century of brilliant inventions it may not be profitless to pause for a moment and inquire how they have affected the well-being of humanity, especially of the teeming inarticulate millions outside the pale of Western civilisation, who constitute the greater portion of mankind.

The more important applications of Natural Science which have affected any considerable section of the human community may be conveniently grouped under the following heads :—

I. The labour-saving machinery which has been so largely utilised in manufacturing, mining, and agricultural industries.

II. The railway, steam navigation, and the electric telegraph, which, by almost annihilating distance, have greatly facilitated trade and intercourse.

III. A variety of inventions like the phonograph, photography, etc., which add to our comforts or refined enjoyments.

IV. Improved guns, rifles, and other munitions of war.

I. Labour-saving machinery may be said to have benefited humanity by cheapening production, and thus placing within the reach of the poorer classes comforts and decencies of life which they could not command before. To a large section of the Orientals, however, the benefit is of a highly questionable character. In the first place, the cheap machine-made articles of the West have destroyed most of their indigenous manufactures. Thus the profits of such manufactures, instead of remaining in the country and enriching it, now go out of it and swell the drain from the East to the West; and the great majority of the artisan populations being suddenly thrown upon agriculture for their livelihood, the pressure upon land has increased considerably, to the serious detriment of the agricultural and labouring classes. The Orientals make faint efforts here and there to compete with the Europeans; but, under present conditions, there is hardly any hope that they will ever be able to do so successfully, except in independent and Europeanised Japan. Depressed by the loss of their independence, total or partial, poorer than the poorest nation of the West, and without any scientific or mechanical training in the Western sense, they have to run a race with a people who have had the start of a century, and who are armed with all the advantages of accumulated capital—not a small portion of which is derived from the exploitation of the East—of long scientific and mechanical training, and of the assurance engendered by conscious strength. As Mr. C. H. Pearson observes in his *National Life and Character* :—

"Let us conceive the leading European nations to be stationary, while the black and yellow Belt, including China, Malaysia, India, Central Africa and Tropical America is all teeming with life, developed by industrial enterprise, fairly well administered by native governments, and owning the greater part of the carrying trade of the world. Can any one suppose that, in such a condition of political society, the habitual temper of mind of Europe would not be profoundly changed? Depression, hopelessness, a disregard of invention and improvement would replace the sanguine confidence of races that at present are always panting for new worlds to conquer."*

Besides ruining the indigenous industries of the East, the cheap and attractive manufactures of the West turned out by labour-saving machinery have generally had the tendency of unduly and prematurely raising the standard of living among peoples brought under Western influence. Men are everywhere ruled more or less by fashion; even the most rational men are found among its most irrational votaries. The desire for show appears to be almost more or less innate in all classes in all parts of the world. Formerly, however, the gratification of this desire among the Orientals was determined by the indigenous standard of comfort and luxury which was well adapted to their material condition. But at the present day there is a marked tendency among the upper and middle classes to adopt the Western standard of necessaries and luxuries. These have been made cheap and attractive by the labour-saving machinery, and therein lies their danger. They are bought more because they are cheap,

* *Op cit.* p. 130.

attractive, and fashionable, than because they are necessary. In the West, modern civilisation has raised the standard of living considerably. There the rise, though fraught with evil consequences, as we shall see hereafter, has been attended by some compensating advantages. In the East, however, the spread of the Western standard of comfort and convenience, without the previous accumulation of wealth and the preparation of mechanical talent as in the West, is an unmitigated evil, and cannot imply progress either present or prospective. The development of Western tastes and Western habits in the Orientals in the present state of their industrial development means, in the case of those few who can afford it, the further enrichment of the already rich capitalist classes of the West and the corresponding impoverishment of the already poor industrial classes in the East; and in the case of those who cannot afford such development—and they are by far the most numerous class—it means also pecuniary embarrassment and possible ruin, the sacrifice of necessaries to luxuries, of substance to shadow.

Not only are the benefits conferred by labour-saving machinery on at least a considerable section of humanity of a questionable character, but they have also to be weighed against positive evils of a serious nature. It is labour-saving machinery which has created and fostered capitalism, one of the greatest curses of the Western social state. No industry on a small scale and with a small capital can be remunerative at the present day. Concentration of capital is the essential condition of industrial development on Western lines, whether manufacturing, mining, or even agricultural, because of the heaviness of the cost of machinery. The success or failure of an industry depends chiefly upon the scale and quality of the machinery, and therefore upon the amount of capital. The larger the capital, the more will it command high-class, expensive machinery, the more consequently will be the profit. So capital begets capital and goes on growing. It is, however, always confined within a small class. True, industries are now mostly conducted by joint-stock organisation, and anybody can have a share in it. But the poorer classes are debarred from the privilege, partly on account of their poverty and partly on account of the speculative character, partaking more or less of the nature of gambling, the most Western enterprises. Thus capital tends to be concentrated within a small section of the richer portions of the community, which has the monopoly of it, and, therefore, of the industries for which it is indispensable. The number of capitalists grows, but in inverse proportion to the number of the wretched poor on the brink of starvation. If in the West the number of millionaires has increased by tens, the number of the abject poor has increased by thousands. The whole world is gradually becoming the theatre of operations of coteries of adventurous and certainly not over-scrupulous Western capitalists. The peoples of the East, and partly also those of the West, are exploited for their benefit. They regulate the wages of the labouring classes, which are everywhere kept at a subsistence figure, control the markets of the world, and to a great extent determine the domestic as well as the foreign policy of the Western Powers. The pugnacious propensity of the Occidental often breaks out in prolonged strikes and determined riots, but the more peace-loving Oriental usually submits to his fate with quiet resignation.

The evils of modern capitalism have been forcibly pointed out by Western writers. In the wake of modern science, marching onward with long and rapid strides, has closely followed in the West poverty of a type hitherto unknown. In the forcible words of Professor Huxley, this poverty is

" a condition in which food, warmth, and clothing, which are necessary for the mere maintenance of the functions of the body in their normal state, cannot be obtained; in which men, women and children are forced to crowd into dens where decency is abolished and the most ordinary conditions of healthful existence are impossible of attainment: in which the pleasures within reach are reduced to brutality and drunkenness: in which the pains accumulate at compound interest in the shape of starvation, disease, stunted development, and moral degradation: in which the prospect of even steady and honest industry is a life of unsuccessful battling with hunger rounded by a Pauper's grave. I take it to be a mere plain truth, that throughout industrial Europe there is not a single large manufacturing city which is free from a large mass of people whose condition is exactly that described, and from a still greater mass, who, living just on the edge of the social swamp, are liable to be precipitated into it."

"About one-third of the total population of London [says Dr. A. R. Wallace] are living miserable poverty-stricken lives, the bulk of them with grinding, hopeless toil, only modified by the still worse conditions of want of employment, with its accompaniments of harassing anxiety and partial starvation. And this is a true picture of what exists in all our great cities and to a somewhat less degree of intensity over the whole country. There is surely very little indication here of any improvement in the condition of the people. Can it be maintained, has it ever been suggested—that in the early part of the century more than one-third of the inhabitants of London did not have sufficient of the bare necessaries of life? In order that there may have been any considerable improvement, an improvement in any degree commensurate with the vast increase of wealth, a full half of the entire population of London must then have lived in this condition of want and misery; and

I am not aware that any writer has ever suggested, much less proved, that such was the case. I believe, myself, that in no earlier period has there been such a large proportion of our population living in absolute want below the margin of poverty, as at the present time."*

As corroborative of this statement, Dr. Wallace cites figures from the reports of the Registrar-General to show that the proportion of deaths in workhouses, hospitals, and in other public institutions for London, and also for England and Wales has been increasing for the last thirty-five years. In 1861—65 the proportion was 16·2 per cent ; in 1892—96 it was 26·2. In England and Wales suicides have increased most alarmingly, from 1,347 in 1861 to 2,796 in 1895, the increase in proportion to population during the same period having been from 67 per million to 92 per million. Crime has increased within the last thirty years, and at a much greater rate than the increase of the population for the same period.

"The evidence for the enormous increase of the total mass of misery and want [says Dr. Wallace] is overwhelming, while that it has increased even faster than the increase of population is, to my own mind, almost equally clear."†

Such is the picture of the preasent condition of the

* *The wonderful Century*, pp. 345-346.

† *The Wonderful Century*, p. 363.

mixed and bound in ties of symathy with them. In the history of the world we have many instances of countries in which the governing classes were naturalised foreigners, and which have made considerable progress in civilisation. India, China and England are conspicuous instances of such countries. But we are not aware of a single country which has left its mark in history under absentee alien rule. Any form of bureaucracy which determines what is supposed to be good for its subjects without consulting their wishes and taking their help—without, in short, closely associating them with it—is not likely to succeed in its purpose. The failure becomes greater and more certain when the bureaucracy is a foreign one, with a civilisation entirely different from that of the people. The truth of this proposition is so ovious that it is incredible it should be so generally forgotten by the Western nations; and that foreign rulers should not associate the people in shaping their administrations. The methods of the political or commercial missionary of the West are such as may well make the realisation of the dream of peace descending in a "drapery of calico," dreamt of by the Manchester politican, as remote as ever. It is, indeed, strange that he should ever seriously think that he is benefiting peoples while he is depleting their resources, giving them shadows while taking away their substan[...] Suppose you take possession of the estate of a person [...] is without your capital and your mechanical knowledg[...] we shall not inquire how. You effectively prevent theft [...] the property, and develop its resources, taking the whole of its yield as the price of your labour and the interest of your capital, except the wages of the proprietors, who work as your labourers. A good portion, if not the whole, of what is left after the cost of their food, is spent upon clothing and little attractive fineries which are manufactured by sections of your community. You do not settle upon the estate, you do not in any way identify yourself with the original proprietors. All the wealth you acquire is spent in a way so as to benefit yourself and your community, except a small fraction of it, which is paid for their labour, which is generally of a menial character. You have, it is true, relieved them of the responsibility of defending the little property they called their own, and even perhaps disburdened them of the arms they possessed. It is possible that, with your fineries which it is your interest to sell them, they assume a more civilised appearance than they ever did before. It is possible that they have, now and then, the comfort of a ride on a railway which you have built, and which you maintain with the proceeds of their estate.

But, notwithstanding all this, can the condition of the original owners be said to be better than when they had freedom, the first condition of progress and happiness, when, though they had to defend their estate against occasional depredations with their own arms and the help of their own people, they had still all the actualities and all the possibilities of real proprietorship ? Would it not be a mockery to tell them that they might compete with you if they liked, knowing very well that they have neither your industrial experience nor your capital—augmented not a little, be it remarked, by the profits from their property—nor the prestige and the numerous other advantages conferred by the possession and administration of their estate. The importance of order as a condition of prosperity must not be exaggerated. As in the case of the individual, so in that of the nation, perfect tranquillity is not incompatible with a state bordering upon lifelessness, the negation, if not the reverse of what is usually understood by progress. The tranquillity maintained by a Government in which the people have a substantial share not only indicates development, but also aids it materially in various ways. But the tranquillity maintained by such an exclusive foreign administration, as has been established by the Europeans in various parts of Asia and Africa, can be neither indicative nor promotive of the well-being of the peoples subject to it.

The speech of the Indian Red-Jacket in answer to a European missionary who went to preach Christianity among the American Indians finds an echo in the hearts of many an Asiatic and African at the present day :

" Brother listen to what we say. There was a time when our forefathers owned this great land. . . . . But an evil day came upon us! Your forefathers crossed the great waters, and landed on this land. Their numbers were small; they found friends and not enemies; they told us they had fled from their own country for fear of wicked men, and came here to enjoy their religion. They asked for a small seat. We took pity on them, granted their request, and they sat down among us. We gave them corn and meat, and they gave us poison (spirituous liquor) in return. The white people had now found out our country, tidings were carried back, and more came amongst us; yet we did not fear them, we took them to be friends; they called us brothers, we believed them and gave them a large seat. At length their numbers had greatly increased, they wanted more land, they wanted our country. Our eyes were opened, and our minds became uneasy. Wars took place; Indians were hired to fight against Indians, and many of our people were destroyed. They also brought strong liquor among us; it was strong and powerful, and has slain thousands.

"Brother, our seats were once large, and yours were very small. You have now become a great people, and we have scarcely a place left to spread our blankets. You have got our country, but are not satisfied—you want to force your religion upon us."*

"Fundamentally [says A. de Quatrefages] the white, even when civilised, from the moral point of view is scarcely better than the negro, and too often by his conduct in the midst of inferior races has justified the argument opposed by a Malagache to a missionary: 'Your soldiers seduce all our women. . . . You come to rob us of our land, pillage the country, and make war against us; and you wish to force your God upon us, saying that He forbids robbery, pillage, and war! Go; you are white upon one side, and black upon another.' Such is the criticism of a savage. The following is that of a European, M. Rose, giving his opinion of his own countrymen: 'The people are simple and confiding when we arrive, perfidious when we leave them. Once sober, brave and honest, we make them drunken, lazy, and finally thieves. After having inoculated them with our vices, we employ these vices as an argument for their destruction.' However severe these conclusions may appear they are unfortunately true, and the history of the relations of Europeans with the populations they have encountered in America, at the Cape, and in Oceania justify them only too fully."†

"The condemnation of our system of rule over tributary states," says Wallace, "is to be plainly seen in plague and famine running riot in India after more than a century of

* Winterbottom's *America*, quoted in *Colonisation and Christianity* by Mr. Howitt, pp. 399—401.

† *The Human Species.* ("International Scientific Series.") Second Edition, pp. 461-462.

British rule and nearly forty years of the supreme power of the English Government. Neither plague nor famine occurs to-day in well-governed communities. That the latter, at all events, is almost chronic in India, a country with an industrious people and a fertile soil, is the direct result of governing in the interests of the ruling classes, instead of making the interests of the governed the first and the only object."*

To quote the same writer, in Africa.

" the result so far has been the sale of vast quantities of rum and gunpowder ; much bloodshed, owing to the objection of the natives to the seizure of their lands and cattle ; great demoralisation of black and white, and the condemnation of the conquered tribes to a modified form of slavery:"†

The application of labour-saving machinery to mining and agricultural industries has, besides contributing to capitalism and over-production, been productive of other evils only a degree less serious. Mining or plantation under modern conditions leads to too quick exhaustion of the mineral or agricultural resources of a country. No thought is given to the future; the present is all that is cared for. One of the strongest arguments adduced in favour of Western expansion is that it develops the backward tracts of the world. The " development," however, is of no advantage what-

The Wonderful Century, pp. 337—340.
† *Op. cit.* p. 372.

ever to the peoples of those tracts, to whom it means loss of independence, the first condition of progress and happiness, and loss of valuable resources. What would have been the present condition of England, France and Germany if they had been "developed" in the earlier centuries of the Christian era in the way in which parts of Asia and Africa, not more backward than they were then, are being developed now? The "development" means only the quick enrichment of a few Western companies at the expense, not only of the interests of large existing communities, but also those of countless future generations.

II. The railway and steam navigation, by promoting friendly intercourse between the East and the West might have knit the bonds of human brotherhood closer, but have tended only to loosen them by facilitating the transport of Western merchandise, Western troops, and Western engines of destruction, and by rendering possible the government or control of tropical and subtropical regions from temperate Europe. Labour-saving machinery could not have done the harm it has done if it had not been helped by cheap and quick means of transit. For then its produce could not have been sent abroad on such an extensive scale as it is now, nor could it have competed with our hand-made manufactures so successfully as it does now, and the European Powers would not have been so eager to possess or control Eastern markets as they are now.

Never before in the history of man was the establishment of such world-wide empires ever attempted as it has been in recent times by the foremost Western Powers. The extent and solidarity of the modern empires are due mainly to the annihilation of distance by steam and electricity. The ancient empires were not only of much smaller extent than those that are being built up at the present day, but the gulf between the conquerors and the conquered was not so wide as it is now. The conquerors generally had to settle in the lands they conquered. Communication with their parent country was either cut off altogether, as in the case of the Aryans in India, or was slow and intermittent, as in the case of the Greeks in Western Asia. Intermarriage between the conquerers and the conquered gradually took place. Alexander married a Persian princess and encouraged his officers and soldiers to intermarry. The bigotry even of the Mohamedan conquerors of India gradually wore off, and several of the Mogul emperors of India took Hindu wives. Thus there was a tendency towards the effacement of the line of demarcation between the conquerors and the conquered, and there sprung up sympathetic relations between them. They gradually came to have common interests, common language, and in a few cases even common religion. The greater majority of the Hindus are the offspring of the Aryan invaders and the non-Aryan aborigines of India, as the English are the descendants of the Saxon and Norman conquerors and the aboriginal population of England.

The object of the Western conqueror or exploiter is to squeeze as much out of the East as possible and enjoy it at home. The facilities afforded by steam communication enable him to do that with ease and comfort. The social barrier between him and the Oriental is impassable. There can be no lasting and real sympathy between them. It is true the European is not unoften actuated by a high sense of duty, and when his own interest or that of his nation is not concerned, tries to do even-handed justice. But duty and justice can never do a fraction of the good that can be done by love and sympathy.

The exclusive policy invariably adopted by the Europeans in their Eastern dependencies is partly due to this want of sympathy, and partly to the fact that these dependencies are regarded by them as so many preserves for various money-making pursuits ; and the moral and economic results of this policy have been most disastrous to the natives. The conquered peoples are, in the words of J. S. Mill,

> " without any potential voice in their own destiny. They exercise no will in respect to their collective interests. All is decided for them by a will not their own, which is legally a crime for them to disobey. What sort of human beings can be formed under such a regimen ? What development can either their thinking or their active faculties attain under it ? A person must have very unusual taste for intellectual exercise in and for itself who will put himself to the trouble of thought when it is to have no outward effect, or to qualify himself for functions which he has no chance of being allowed to exercise."*

The Eastern dependencies of the Western Powers are being slowly drained of their wealth in the shape of the pay and pension of Western troops and Western officers, civil and military ; dividends of the numerous Western companies, profits of Western merchants, etc. This ceaseless and ever-increasing drain, though slow, does, on the whole, incomparably more harm than the occasional though violent depredations of former invaders ever did, just as the almost imperceptible but continuous operation of rainwater, frost and wind does far more

* *Considerations on Representative Government*, chap. iii.

serious havoc to the crust of the earth than such cataclysmal convulsions as earthquakes and volcanic eruptions.

III. One of the most important effects of the inumerable inventions for gratifying our senses has been to multiply our wants and raise the standard of living, and thus to intensify the struggle for existence. The animal necessities of life render a certain amount of struggle almost inevitable. But the object of true progress should be to minimise, not to increase it. The more our energies are absorbed by it, the less room there is for their employment in the higher struggle of the soul for the attainment of a better condition. In ancient times, and, indeed, until recently, the spiritual interest of man was generally held to be antagonistic to his worldly interests. Exaltation of the spiritual nature at the expense of the animal was held up as the ideal of human perfection. But the ideal of modern civilisation is material progress, and there is no doubt that it is greatly furthered by the incessant strife and stress necessitated by the continual elevation of the standard of necessaries and luxuries. This progress, however, practically means accumulation of wealth by only a small section of the Western community by the exploitation, impoverishment, and virtual enthralment of the weak and helpless peoples of Asia and Africa; and it is almost incomprehensible to us that such an object should be considered by Western States to be worth such a sacrifice.

Continuous increase of luxury, besides the moral degeneration to which it inevitably leads sooner or later, is attended by other evil consequences of a serious nature. It is undeniable that a large number of the Western working-men are now better lodged, better fed and better clothed than they were half a century ago, but the gulf between their material condition and that of their masters is wider than ever. The relative poverty of the Western working-man has increased where his actual poverty has not. Therein lies the secret of the growing discontent and restlessness even among the comparatively well-to-do labouring classes in Europe. The increase of luxury naturally begins at the top of the social scale. When a desire for it reaches the bottom, as it must do sooner or later, there is heart-burning. With every addition to the wealth and luxury of the upper classes, unless there be a corresponding addition to the wealth and luxury of the lower classes, the latter will be discontented, and will clamour for a rise in their wages and for shorter working hours. After a period of loss and anxiety on the side of the Haves, and of misery and probably also barbarity on the side of the Have-nots, the dispute between them is compromised, but never satisfactorily settled. As the standard of luxury is perpetually rising in the West, the struggle between Capital and Labour is perpetually recurring.

IV. The influence of the numerous improvements effected in arms and ammunition by modern science has been highly detrimental to the well-being of mankind in general and of the Asiatics and Africans in particular. That the Western nations are becoming alive to a sense of their injurious tendency is shown by the following suggestions from the Czar which were put forward for discussion at the first International Conference held at the Hague :

1. To prohibit the use in armies and fleets of any new kind of firearms whatever, and of new explosives, or any powders more powerful than those now in use either for rifles or cannon.

2. To restrict the use in military warfare of the formidable explosives already existing, and prohibit the throwing of projectiles or explosives of any kind from balloons or by any similar means.

3. To prohibit the use in naval warfare of submarine torpedo-boats or plungers, or other similar engines of

destruction, and to give an undertaking not to construct vessels with rams in future.

Might has always been right in this world. But the improved arms of long range and precision, and the explosives which have so largely come into use in recent times, have made might much mightier than ever before. The weak and ignorant have always been more or less oppressed or exploited by the strong and knowing, but never so extensively, fearlessly, and systematically as at the present day. The unscientific people of the world do not now appear to have any other prospect before them than that of hopeless and helpless bondage. They are now entirely at the mercy of the scientific people of the West, except where their independence is secured by difficult mountain fastnesses. Science, however, may yet overcome such natural barriers ; and flying cars may one day transport over them Western troops and Western merchandise.

Thus we see that Western science, instead of being the blessing which it was expected and is still supposed to be, has on the whole proved to be rather a curse to large sections of the human race. If it had not been so extensively applied to practical purposes for saving labour, for adding to comforts and luxuries, and for increasing the destructiveness of firearms ; if its cultivation had been more confined within the limits of intellectual culture, it would not only have done no harm ; but would probably have done an immense amount of good. But its mechanical applications, which are considered by Western writers as its chief title to commendation, are to our mind its chief title to condemnation.

The characteristic feature of the modern progress of the West is the great prominence which it gives to Natural Science, especially to its industrial applications. The intellectual basis of the Eastern civilisations, on the other hand, was mental and moral philosophy. The aim of natural Science, or Western Scince as we shall call it, is much the same as that of Eastern philosophy—the good or well being of humanity. But they differ fundamentally in their conception of the good, and the way in which it is to be accomplished. In Eastern especially Indian, philosophy, it is spiritual or ethical development for which, among other things, a life of more or less ascetic simplicity is requisite. In this respect, it is at one with the Greek or Roman philosophy. No Hindu teacher could have exhorted his disciples to be independent of external circumstances and bodily conditions more forcibly or more earnestly than did the Socratic or the Stoic sage. Even Epicurus, with whom pleasure was the sole ultimate good, maintained the immense superiority of the pleasures of the mind over those of the body, and the Epicurean sage no less than the Vedantic sought for happiness and tranquillity of soul from within rather than from without. The ancient philosopher, Eastern as well as Western, strove to keep the struggle for animal existence to the lowest point of animal necessity in order that one might be free, so far as possible, from the moral corruption incidental to it, and might, if he chose, devote more time and energy to the higher and more arduous struggle for spiritual development than he would otherwise be able to do.

The ascetic tendencies of ancient philosophy were detrimental to mechanical and industrial development to any great extent. The mathematical and physical sciences were not neglected. They were, however, cultivated not as parents of useful arts, but as aids to culture and devotion. The attitude of the ancient philosophers in this respect is well illustrated, though in a somewhat exaggerated manner, by Plato, who valued mathematics chiefly, if not solely, because it accustomed the mind to the contemplation of eternal truth, and who remonstrated with his friend Archytas for inventing machines of extraordinary power.

It is far otherwise with the Western Science of the

present day. It takes but little account of spiritual or ethical life, and seeks to accomplish the well-being of man by mechanical and industrial development, by adding to his comforts and conveniences, by multiplying his wants and desires. One of the most important consequences of this rapid and ceaseless mechanical elaboration and material progress of the age has been to continually raise the standard of comfort in the West, so that what was looked upon as luxury fifty years ago would be barely considered as necessity now; and this has had the effect of spreading discontent, and of immensely intensifying and embittering the struggle for existence among the peoples of the West.

Western scientists are constantly dinning into our ears that the increase of population is the main, if not the sole, cause of the starvation, misery and untimely extinction of a large portion of it. A doctrine more mischievous in its effects or less founded in fact could hardly be conceived. The world has existed for thousands of years, and the pressure of population has never been too much for it. It was not the increase of population in Macedon or France that made Alexander or Napoleon burn for territorial expansion. No, It is vanity, ambition, or inordinate desire for the accumulation of wealth that has ever led the strong, the cunning and the greedy to exploit, oppress, enslave, or decimate the weak and the simple. There was room enough and to spare in America, Australia and Africa for European colonisation, without exterminating or enthralling the simple and, in not a few cases, confiding aborigines, if the European had been less actuated by an unquenchable thirst for material aggrandisement. There is room enough even now in Europe for much further expansion of its peoples if only they were intent upon living more in conformity with the high ethical standard of the noble religion they profess, and were content to lead comparatively simple lives. They would not then need to pursue a career of spoliation, euphemistically called Imperial Expansion, on the pretence of spreading their civilisation among peoples who feel that they can get on well enough, and perhaps even much better, without them.

But the mechanical progress of the age has rendered a simple ethical life almost an impossibility in the West. Work under modern Western conditions with railways, telegraphs, telephones, and a multitude of other ingenious contrivances for condensing a large amount of work within a small amount of time, causes a wear and tear of the nervous system, the reparation of which necessitates a rather high standard of living ; and an infinity of inventions for the gratification of our senses fosters and promotes it. As there is no limit to mechanical development, there is also no limit to the elevation of the standard of living ; and ceaseless rise of this standard implies equally ceaseless struggle for the acquisition and accumulation of wealth. Mechanical elaboration has also contributed to the intensity of this struggle by making concentration of capital an indispensable condition of industrial development and commercial expansion on which Western civilisation rests. There has never been a community of any size which has emerged out of the primitive stage of existence in which certain sections have not been ardent votaries of Mammon. But there never has been a civilised society in which Mammonism has been so universally prevalent as in the Western social state of the present day. The high born as well as the low-born, the educated and cultured as well as the uneducated and ignorant, all are eagerly engaged in the insane race for wealth ; and in that motley group there may occasionally be recognised even ministers of religion who know or should know better than other people, that it would be easier for a camel to go through the eye of a needle than for a rich man to enter the kingdom of heaven. They cannot resist the influence of their environment. They can no more help being carried along by the tide of material progress than a piece of floating wood can help being drifted by the rushing stream. The manifold evils to which Mammonism has given rise in Western society are too well known to need recounting here ; and if they were confined to the West we would watch what we (Asiatics) consider the misguided efforts of our occidental brother for material aggrandisment with sorrow or commiseration. But the same science which has been impelling him to these efforts has, by annihilating distance and placing in his hands diabolic weapons of destruction, enabled him to successfully carry his operations to every quarter of the globe ; and his conduct among the peoples outside the pale of western civilisation sometimes awakens in us feelings which make us shudder.

But is he not among those peoples on a benevolent mission of progress and civilisation ? That is the "flattering unction" which he would fain lay to his soul, though I can almost see the lips of the cynical statesman curling into a sardonic smile as he gives vent to such platitudes from the platform. Can any well-informed occidental seriously think that he is benefiting peoples while he is crushing their independence, smothering their aspirations, destroying their indigenous industries, recklessly and remorselessly depleting their resources for his own benefit, inoculating them with Western vices, and making them "hewers of wood and drawers of water," if not reducing them to a condition undistinguishable from that of bondage? Can he honestly believe that he is ever likely to substantially and permanently benefit peoples whom he hardly ever understands or cares to understand, except as objects of exploitation and with whom he can, therefore, seldom sympathise?

The immoral tendencies of the material development promoted by the practical applications of Western Science have been deepened and strengthened by the theory of the "survival of the fittest," which of late has obtained such prominence in Western thought. Instead of being looked upon as a mere hypothesis to account for the genesis of specific forms, it has come also to be regarded, though most illogically, as if it were a doctrine in conformity with which man should live and should behave towards his fellow-man. No biologist of note would openly countenance such a monstrous perversion of his favourite theory. He would be the first to point out, that the "fittest" who may survive in the struggle for existence, whether it be the individual or the nation, may not be ethically the best, but, on the contrary, may often be the very reverse. But, all the same,

Western society is so deeply imbued with the evolutional, which has come to be synonymous with the gladiatorial, view of life, that its estimation of moral qualities is becoming more and more dependent upon the measure of cosmic success to which they may contribute. It is forgotten that wordly prosperity is so seldom and so inadequately apportioned to moral worth, that the cross may almost be said to be emblematic of the life of the good in this world. The moral standard of evolutional ethics estimates actions by their conduciveness to the "efficiency of the social organism." The ideal indicated by such an utilitarian standard must necessarily be a low one. It tends to develop a certain amount of what may be called commercial honesty and truthfulness, and such qualities as industry and preserverance which should be regarded as qualities only so long as they are not misdirected, but which in the latter case stunt the growth of the higher virtues of self-sacrificing benevolence, charity and mercy. "Ideal conduct," says Herbert Spencer, "is not possible for the ideal man in the midst of men otherwise constituted. An absolutely just or perfectly sympathetic person could not live and act according to his nature in a tribe of cannibals. Among peoples who are treacherous and utterly without scruple, entire truthfulness and openness must bring ruin. If all around recognise only the law of the strongest, one whose nature will not allow him to inflict pain on others must go to the wall. There requires a certain congruity between the conduct of each member of a society and others' conduct. A mode of action entirely alien to the prevailing modes of action cannot be successfully persisted in—must eventuate in death to itself, or posterity, or both." ("Principles of Ethics," part I., ch. XV.). Conformity to a standard of morality indicated by these propositions would result, under existing Western conditions, in a community composed of individuals who would ceaselessly and energetically struggle for the acquisition of wealth, not much hampered by qualms of conscience, who would exploit weaker individuals, classes or races, and reduce them, where possible, to a condition of virtual slavery, and who would be as alert to perceive a wrong as prompt to avenge it.

The ancient line of demarcation between this-worldliness and other-worldliness, between the animal and the spiritual, is not recognisable in the Western moral system of the present day. The moral precepts of antiquity are, it is true, not discarded. But they are interpreted so as to serve the purpose of social efficiency, and are hedged in with qualifications and restrictions which render them practically inoperative as ideals of moral conduct. The New Testament is the recognised moral guide of the Western world, but its cardinal principles are so uniformly and systematically disregarded that they might as well have been erased. Christianity with its high ideal of self-sacrifice and benevolence, cannot harmonise with the commercial spirit of an industrial civilisation like the Western. If a Christ or a Buddha were to appear now in the West, he would be ridiculed as a visionary by most people. He would not even be considered real enough to be worth persecuting.

Even a philosophic and cultured scientist like the late Professor Huxley, who could not but be fully acquainted with the arduous nature of the struggle for moral development, and the inherent antagonism between it and the struggle for material progress, was so much under the influence of his Western environment, that he viewed the attempts to attain tranquillity and salvation, whether Greek or Indian, which "ended in flight from the battle-field" as the "youthful discouragement of nonage." He would have the Europeans of the present day as

"grown men, play the man,
Strong in will
To strive, to seek, to find and not to yield."

("Evolution and Ethics.")

Man may have been evolved out of lower animals, but for a philosophic biologist like Huxley to assert that man at the present day is "grown man" as compared with man two or three thousand years ago is to assert something for which there is not a scintilla of scientific evidence. Intellectually or morally man is no better now than he was then. The intellectual calibre of a Cuvier or Darwin cannot certainly be said to be superior to that of an Aristotle or Kapila, and as regards ethical development, it would be almost heresy to compare the present with the age that produced a Buddha or Christ. If the ancient sages counselled retirement from the strife and stress of material progress so far as practicable, it was because the greater and more arduous battle of spiritual progress might be fought more energetically and efficaciously, because they held with Buddha.

> " One may conquer a thousand thousand men in battle,
> But he who conquers himself is the greatest victor."

The Western nations are " playing the man," " to strive, to seek, to find"—to find what ? Not the victory which is achieved by love, mercy and self-sacrifice, but the victory, the path to which lies over broken hearts, if not also over broken heads, over the misery, starvation and destruction of countless fellow-creatures in all quarters of the globe.

The phenomenal mechanical progress of the age has dealt a death-blow to what used to be called cottage industries. No industry on a small scale with a small capital can be remunerative at the present day. Concentration of capital, or capitalism, is the essential condition as well as the necessary consequence of Western industrial development; and capitalism is decidedly not making for moral progress. It has substituted urban for unquestionably healthier rural conditions of life, and has led to enormous inequality in the distribution of wealth. The increase in the number of Western millionaires with fabulous wealth has been remarkable, but the increase in the number of the abject poor sunk in the lowest depths of vice and misery has been still more remarkable. The evils of modern capitalism are, indeed, often pointedly referred to—nay, forcibly descanted upon by Western writers. It seems to us strange, however, that they should be blind to the root cause of the evil—the progress of Natural Science; so much so, indeed, that in the same breath will they anathematise the nefarious practices of unscrupulous capitalists and extol the wonderful triumphs of modern science—the very triumphs which create and foster capitalism.

The nature of man may originally have been all good,

but, as found at present, it is a curious compound of good and evil. The work of true progress should be to suppress the one and develop the other. The material progress of the West is certainly not doing this. On the contrary, its tendency has been to give an impetus to the evil impulses of human nature. We have seen how it is responsible for the adoption of a low standard of morality which may be called the morality of expediency; and this morality is becoming more and more marked in the literature and conduct of the Western nations. The doctrine enunciated by Rumelin, that "the maintenance of the State is superior to every moral rule," is the doctrine which is being more and more largely adopted by every power in the West. The military spirit, which is always prejudical to true progress, is becoming more and more rampant all over Europe. It has invaded even the clerical, literary and scientific classes. There are warlike luminaries of science and literature as there are militant dignitaries of the Christian church, who from their pulpits invoke the aid and blessing of Heaven on aggressive wars involving the wanton destruction of thousands of fellow-creatures. The armaments of Europe have been increasing apace, and will continue to increase, so long as mechanical science dominates Western civilisation, and material progress continues to be its goal. The great Powers of the West have entered into a compact to partition Asia and Africa among them—a compact not less real because it is not formal, not less immoral because it is necessitated by the pressure of material progress. Markets must be opened up and controlled for the produce of the gigantic mills and factories of the West, outlets must be found for Western enterprise—the whole world must be converted into a happy hunting ground of adventurous and certainly not over-scrupulous Western capitalists. Despotism has joined hands with Republicanism, Liberalism with Conservatism, and Protestantism with Catholicism in the cause of Western expansion and Western domination in eastern climes. Nations which were once foremost in promoting liberty and equality are now busiest in forging chains of thraldom for the weak and helpless peoples of Asia and Africa.

Natural Science on its theoretical side has done most commendable work. It has created several new branches of science, and widened and illumined others. On its practical side also, in medicine and surgery its effect has been to alleviate human misery. But the good thus conferred is confined to a comparatively insignificant fraction of humanity, and is far outweighed by the evils wrought by the practical applications of Physics and Chemistry. It is said that Archimedes was half ashamed of those wonderful inventions of his which were the admiration of his age. If modern science were more actuated by this ancient spirit, if it had not lent its aid so largely to material progress, and had kept more within the bounds of intellectual culture and ethical development, we would have almost unqualified praise for it. But its mechanical applications, which from such a fertile them for exuberant jubilation in the West, arouse in us only feelings of anxiety and apprehension.

CHAPTER VI

CHHATTISGAR : NOTES ON ITS TRIBES, SECTS AND CASTES

(Extract from the Journal, Asiatic Society of Bengal Vol. LIX, pt. 10, 1890)

§ 1. A brief account of Chhattisgar

THE Bengal-Nagpur Railway will open up a tract of country which is now but little known to the public. In the Central Provinces, it is called "Chhattisgar." Two derivations of the name have been proposed. According to the Central Provinces Gazetteer,* Chhattisgar owes its name to thirty-six (*chhattis*) forts (*gar*) included within it. Serious objections, however, have been urged against this interpretation by Mr. Beglar of the Archæological Survey.† While in Behar he heard a tradition, that ages ago, in the

* *Op. cit.*, p. 88.

† Arch. Surv. Rep. Vol. VII.

time of Jarásandha, thirty-six families of chámárs had emigrated from that country and settled in a country far to the south of it, which was called "Chhattisgar" (thirty-six families). He was not at the time aware of any country which bore that name, and his inquiries with regard to it being ineffectual, he became rather sceptical about its existence. When, however, official duty brought him to Chhattisgar, the tradition he had heard in Behar came back to his mind. Here was a country far from Behar, and south of it, the people of which appeared to him to be singularly like the Beharis in language, dress, manners, and customs—a people, too, of which the chámárs formed a very important element. Mr. Beglar suggests that Chhattisgar derives its name from the thirty-six families of Behari chámárs who settled there; according to which interpretation 'Chhattisgar' should be spelt 'Chhattisghar.' Considering, that long intercourse had made Mr. Beglar perfectly familiar with the Beharis before he visited Chhattisgar, his interpretation becomes authoritative. Besides, it promises to throw some light on the history and affinities of one of the most remarkable peoples that inhabit India—the Chhattisgari chámárs. We must say, however, that as the word is pronounced by the people, it is difficult to make out whether "Chhattisghar" or "Chhattisgar" is the correct spelling; we have adopted the latter as the one in current use.

Physical and political Geography.—Chhattisgar as an administrative division of the Central Provinces comprises the districts of Raipur, Bilaspur and Sambalpur, and including Bastar, covers an area of about 53,000 square miles. But Chhattisgar proper includes Raipur and Bilaspur only; and we shall use the term in this restricted sense. It comprises a central plain covering an area of about 10,000 square miles surrounded by a forest-clad hilly country of a somewhat wider extent (about 12,000 square miles); strictly speaking, the plain country alone should be called Chhattisgar, and it is only for the sake of convenience that we have included the surrounding hill tract within it. The contrast between the hill and the plain country is sharp and striking. The former is clothed with thick jungle, little cultivated, and sparsely populated, the population consisting chiefly of aboriginal tribes. To the *shikari*, it affords sport in abundance; the tiger is especially abundant in the southern, and the wild buffalo in the eastern jungles, while in every direction, the antelope, the spotted deer, and other varieties of game may be found. The plain, on the other hand, is almost flat, perfectly denuded of jungle, well cultivated, and thickly populated. With the exception of a small narrow strip in the western portion, it is what is called *khalsa*, that is, under the direct management of the British Government. The hill tracts are partitioned amongst a number of zamindars and feudatory chiefs, who pay an annual tribute. The zamindars maintain their own police. The feudatory chiefs, whose gross revenue in most cases does not exceed that of second-class zamindars in Bengal, are invested with authority almost equal to that of a Holkar or Nizam. They not only keep their own police, but also have their Jails and civil and criminal courts.

Geology and mineral resources.—The configuration of the country well illustrates the intimate connection between geological structure and physical features: The plain is formed of Vindhyan sandstones, marls and limestones, which have been but little disturbed from their normal horizontal position. The hills surrounding it are, on the other hand, composed of older rocks which have undergone considerable disturbance and metamorphism. At the north-eastern extremity, about Korba there is a considerable outcrop of the coal-bearing strata (Gondwana System). The results of the coal-exploration conducted by the Geological Survey are not very encouraging with regard to the ground traversed.

by the Bengal-Nagpur railway ; but, not very far from it, there is one tract near Korba where workable coal of good quality has been found. In the hills to the north, west, and south extensive iron-ores of exceptionally good quality exist. Iron-smelting is still carried on there to some extent in the primitive fashion. But with the opening of the railway, the industry already on the wane, will probably be nearly extinct. Copper and lead-ores exist ; but their extent is not yet known. The sandstones of the plain are largely used for building purposes ; and the limestones are quarried chiefly for road metal. In places the limestone is tolerably pure and would yield lime of good quality.

Jungle produce.—Of forest produce, lac and *Hurra* (Haritaki, *Terminalia citrina*) are the most important. The former flourishes best on Kusam (*Carthamus tinfosius*) and Palás (*Butea frondosa)*. But it is also grown, though to a very subordinate extent, on Baer (*Ziziphus jujuba*) and a few other trees. The lac is mostly taken to Mirzapur. The *Hurra* is exported to Europe, through Bombay.

Agriculture.—Chhattisgar is, or rather has been the land of plenty. To the people of the neighbouring districts, it has long been known as *khalauti,* or the

"Land of the Threshing-floors." Rice, wheat, and linseed are the chief crops. Rice and wheat were formerly sold—and that too not so very long ago—at fabulously cheap prices. Only five or six years ago, after the opening of the Nagpur-Chhattisgar Railway, rice used to be sold, at some distance from its terminus at Nandgaon, for Re. 1-4 or less per maund. But the price in 1889 was Rs. 2-8, and will no doubt go up still higher when the Bengal-Nagpur Railway system is completed.

In the southern and eastern portion of Raipur, as well as in Bilaspur generally, rice is the principal crop. In the western portion of the plain, wheat appears to be more largely grown than rice. Wherever there is black soil (*kanhar*) wheat is preferably sown on it; whereas rice is chiefly grown on sandy soil. Rice, however, is the principal crop. The area on which rice is grown in the districts of Raipur and Bilaspur amounts to nearly two million acres, whereas the wheat area does not amount to more than 130,000 acres.

History.—The earliest traces of man we found in this district are some bone and pottery mounds by the Seonath river. They invariably occur in the plain country. Who the men were it is difficult to surmise. But, whoever they were, they had passed the stone age, and had been in the habit of using iron implements*. In the south-western portion of the district of Raipur, away in the jungles, there are remains of rude forts and temples which tradition ascribes to a race of Gauli kings. No reliable information, however, is available about them. To a later period, belong the ruined temples and *Sati* pillars of Balod, Gurur, Sirpur &c., some of which date back to the beginning of the Christian era. Mr. Beglar of the Archæological Survey finds evidence in an inscription of the extension of the Chalukya power right into the heart of the modern district of Raipur.

The authentic history of Chhattisgar dates back only to the middle of the eighth century, when Raja Suradeva of the well known Haihai family ruled at Ratanpur† in the district of Bilaspur. The place is now overgrown with jungle; but, extensive tanks and ruins testify to its former grandeur. Nineteen kings of the Haihai line had preceded Suradeva, but all that is known about them is of the vaguest character. Surrounded by barriers of high hills on all sides, Chhattisgar entirely

* Arch. Surv. Rep. Vol. VII. p. 141.

† Central Provinces Gazeteer, p. 90. Mr. Beglar would not allow this town any greater antiquity than the middle of the 15th century. (*Op. cit.*, p. 165).

escaped the Muhammadan invasion, and the Haihai dynasty ruled undisturbed till the middle of the eighteenth century when the country came under the sway of the Bhonslas of Nagpur.

Of less antiquity than the Haihaibansi rulers of Ratanpur were the Gond kings of Garha Mandla, Lanji and Chanda. The western portion of Chhattisgar, included in the zamindaries of Sahuspur-Lohara, Gandai, Doundi-Lohara, &c. belonged to one or other of these dynasties.

In 1818, Chhattisgar came under the superintendence of British officers; and in 1854, on the lapse of the province of Nagpur to the British Government, it was formed into a Deputy Commissionership with head quarters at Raipur. Since then a separate Deputy Commissionership has been established for Bilaspur.

§ 2. General remarks on the tribes, &c.

I have left out the higher Hindu castes, Bráhmans, Rájputs, Káyasthas and Beniyás; the Muhammadans too and such castes as Dhobi, Mehter, &c., who are chiefly met with in towns, have been omitted from these notes as they do not present any special features of interest, being settlers from Northern or Western India. Even of the specially Chhattisgari people, these notes do not pretend to be exhaustive, as they treat of those only with whom I came into personal contact. In thus restricting myself I hoped to have avoided errors into which second-hand information often leads,* and to have attained correctness by sacrificing completeness.

The people, as elsewhere in India, may be broadly divided into Aryan and non-Aryan, or, perhaps less logically into Hindu and Aboriginal. Either of these methods of classification would answer well when we have to deal with such well-marked Aryan or Hindu castes, as Bráhmans, Káyasthas, and Beniyás, on the one hand, or such well marked non-Aryan or Aboriginal people as the Jungly Gonds on the other. But, it is difficult exactly to define the ethnological position of a good many of the castes treated of in these notes. The chámárs, for instance, one of the

* I may illustrate this by an instance, which will be referred to later on. The Central Provinces Gazetteer (to which I am greatly indebted) describes the caste of Hálvás to be distillers ; and Sherring quotes this description in his great work on "Hindu Tribes and Castes," (Vol. II., p. 147). I did not, however, come across a single Hálvá who was a distiller ; and I was told, that there was no such Hálvá in Chhattisgar or anywhere else. There is, however, a clan of the Telis called Háliás, who are distillers by profession. It is this similarity of name which probably led to the confusion.

largest and most interesting castes in Chhattisgar are looked down upon by the Hindus, and in their faith they are rather aggressively anti-Hindu—the word Hindu being used in its popular senses. Yet, physically the chámárs resemble their Aryan more than their non-Aryan neighbours ; and it is impossible to place them in either of these categories without giving rise to serious objections. Similar difficulties are experienced in classifying such castes as the Kanwárs the Pankás and Hálvás. In the present state of our knowledge a rigid system of classification would, I think, be rather disadvantageous than otherwise ; I have not, therefore, adopted any. I may, however, mention in passing, that the Gonds have unquestionable Dravidian affinities, and that the Bhunjiyas, the Baigás, the Komárs, and the Saonras probably belong to the Kolarian group. Whether the Sudra castes such as the Telis, the Márárs, the Koshtás &c., are Aryan or non-Aryan, or a mixture of the two, it is difficult to say exactly. I do not think any of them is of purely Aryan blood, some of them may be Hinduised non-Aryans. The process of transformation is still going on. The greater number of the Gonds who have settled in the plain country amongst the Hindus have adopted the manners and customs of the latter. They are proud to be called Hindus, and are ashamed to own affinity with their brethren of the jungles ; and some few have succeeded so far as to be recognised as Hindus. Some of the castes are probably of mixed descent. The Dhur Gonds appear to be such.

Some castes or sub-castes are due solely to differences of habitat and environment : others to inequality of social position. The castes into which the Gonds are sub divided seem to be mostly explicable by one or other of these causes. Those who have settled in the plains have been greatly affected by their Hindu environment. They have entirely forgotten their own language, have taken to Hindu manners and customs ; and will on no account have social intercourse with their brethren in the jungles. Thus we have two great castes, one comprising settlers in the plain country, and the other dwellers in the jungles. Amongst these, again, minor castes would be formed owing to geographical and social causes. A barrier, such as a range of hills, would prevent intercommunication and social intercorse and give rise to castes. People of high social position, those, for instance, who claim kinship with the once powerful Gond kings of Garha Mandla, Lanji &c., would not associate with those of an inferior status, and would thus form a caste by themselves.

The sects of the Satnamis, the Kabirpanthis and the

Man Bhaus are very interesting. The followers of the of the last named sect were not separately entered at the last census ; they are not, in fact, mentioned. This is an omission which it may be hoped, will not recur at the next census. In the districts of Raipur and Bilaspur the Kabirpanthis number 230,526 and the satnamis 356,533. At the last census the population of these districts including Hindus, and Aborigines, numbered nearly three millions. The Kabirpanthis and the Satnamis, therefore, together form about 24 per cent. of the entire population. The Kabirpanthis do not appear to believe in any God beyond their Guru to whom they accord divine honours. The Marars and the Bhunjiyas also did not express their belief in any God. They have *sthápands* in their houses for their ancestors to whom they give offerings periodically.

The Satnamis are Monotheists, but like the Kabirpanthis they worship their Guru. The Man Bhaus are Vaishnavas.

All these sects, the Kabirpanthis, the Satnamis and the Man Bhaus, abjure caste and eschew flesh and fish and spirituous liquors. A section of the Satnamis abstain even from smoking.

Rice is the principal food of the people in the plain country, and *kodo* that of the Gonds and other tribes living in the jungles. Spirituous liquor (prepared from mhowa flower) is indulged in chiefly by the Gonds, especially those who live in the jungles.

The clothing of men is usually of the scantiest possible dimensions; but, that of women is, as a rule, ample and decorous. In the interior, strong, coarse, indigenous cloth is still largely in use; but with the extension of railways it is to a large extent giving way to cheaper, more showy, though less durable cloth of Manchester make. The fate of the weaving castes like that of the iron-smelters is sealed.

There are certain practices which are common to most of the tribes and castes described in this paper, and which may be conveniently mentioned here.

Re-marriage of widows is a general practice. A widow is allowed to wed herself to the younger brother of her deceased husband—a custom which appears to have largely prevailed in ancient India. She can, however, marry almost anybody she pleases in her own caste. The essential part of the ceremony of such marriage consisting, I am told, in making presents of *churis* (thin glass or earthen bracelets) to the bride—who, in her widowed condition, remains without any ornaments whatever—it is called *churi* marriage. Being inexpensive, it is often resorted to by impecunious wife-hunters in preference to regular marriage which is rather costly. Marriage is certainly not allowed to be a failure in Chhattisgar. A man can of course take to himself as many wives as his means will allow ; and a wife can leave her lord for anybody else provided the latter compensates the injured husband, the damages being rated according to the customary marriage expenses of the caste.

The practice of worshipping the Thakur Deo and Mata is almost universal. The former is the village god, and is worshipped by all the villagers twice a year, in the months of Paus and Chaitra. The Deo consists of a collection of peculiarly shaped stones usually placed on a sort of *dais* under an umbrageous tree. In Drug Subdivision (Raipur district), stool-shaped stones with two legs (supposed by General Cunningham to be Buddhist remains) take the place of the Thakur Deo. Elsewhere, he is supposed to be embodied in characteristically shaped pebbles. Besides the stones strictly representing the Thakur Deo, numbers of others are placed by their side. In fact, the seat of the Thakur Deo is a sort of local museum. Any curiosities found in the neighbourhood, either pebbles or other rock specimens or remains of old temples &c. are carefully deposited there. Before leaving a village, I always made it a point to pay my respects to the Thakur Deo and the visit was always interesting, and sometimes instructive as well.

The worship of the Thakur Deo consists in sacrificing goats and fowls. and having a good feast. In some villages the headman (*malguzar*) collects subscriptions from the villagers, and the expenses of the festival are met from the fund so raised.

Mátá, called also Bhavâni and Kálikâ at places is the well known goddess of smallpox. She is greatly dreaded, and universally worshipped, being carefully lodged in a thatched shed in the outskirts of the village. She is usually represented by a pebble; a trident, an earthen lamp, and a pot for milk or water being its necessary adjuncts. She is worshipped in Baisakh with sacrifices of fowls.

Bhim Sen represented by his celebrated club, a large piece of stone daubed with vermilion, is universally venerated. Mr. Hislop says* that "his worship is spread over all parts of the country, from Berar to the extreme east of Bastar, and that not merely among the Hinduised aborigines, who have begun to honour Khandoba, Hanumán, Ganpati, &c. but among the

* Op. Cit. p. 16.

rudest and most savage of the tribe." This universal popularity of Bhim Sen (who can not be any other than the well known Pándava) is a rather curious fact.

Belief in witchcraft is universal. People coming from Jabalpur and other places are in mortal terror of the Chhattisgaris who are supposed to be past masters in the black art. A Jabalpur servant of mine—a Christian to boot—would ascribe his fever from which he suffered greatly to the malice of a fellow Chhattisgari servant. I have been told many stories about the doings of supposed witches. At one time they were punished by the villagers rather heavily, but since the establishment of British rule, the witches have had a rather easy time of it.

THE END.